HORRIBLE HISTORIES

ROTTEN RULERS

TERRY DEARY

ILLUSTRATED BY MIKE PHILLIPS

D0289600

■SCHOLASTIC

For Bruce Todd

Scholastic Children's Books,
Commonwealth House, 1–19 New Oxford Street
London WC1A 1NU, UK

A division of Scholastic Ltd
London ~ New York ~ Toronto ~ Sydney ~ Auckland
Mexico City ~ New Delhi ~ Hong Kong

Published in the UK by Scholastic Ltd, 2005

Text copyright © Terry Deary, 2005
Illustrations copyright © Mike Phillips, 2005

ISBN 0 439 959365

CONTENTS

INTRODUCTION

Some of the most horrible people in history have been the people in charge. The bosses. The rulers.

You know the sort of people I mean – emperors, kings and queens, warlords and history teachers.

Why are they so horrible? Is it:

A: Being a leader makes you lousy?

Do they get to the top and turn more horrible than a putrid pork pie?

Henry VIII of England was a popular young prince. But once the crown was on his big head he turned nasty. He didn't just have his enemies executed – he also had his old *friends* chopped and a couple of his wives lopped. Horrible.

Or is it:

B: Being lousy makes you a leader?

Are they nasty kids who don't want to grow up?

Caligula used to torture his slaves when he was a boy. When he grew up he liked to have people executed as slowly and painfully as possible. Caligula even invited their parents along to watch the execution. Horrible.

If it is B then rulers are born nasty – so you will probably make a good leader.

After all, you are pretty horrible, aren't you?

Yes, you, dear reader. You must be pretty horrible to be reading a *Horrible Histories* book.

Tests have shown that the average *Horrible Histories* reader is 74.3% more evil than the average reader. Sadly you are also 82.9% uglier as well. You can't have everything. Let's be honest, you would make a great leader.

All you need are a few tips. You need to read about the most monstrous men and wicked women who made it to the top. Learn from their hideous habits – and their miserable mistakes.

You've come to the right book, your highness.

Yes, you too could be the new Nero! He had his wife executed and her dead head sent to his new girlfriend.

You could be the next Nebuchadnezzar – who had his enemies executed and their corpses trampled to mush! He rode a lion with a tame snake wrapped around its neck...

You could be the modern Maximilien Robespierre, whose government sent 1,285 people to the guillotine in six weeks in 1794.

Just one little word of warning:
  A lot of lousy leaders end up dying in painful pieces.[1]

1 Yes, all right, if you want to be picky that is just 12 little words of warning. Just get on with reading the book.

POTTY FOR POWER

So you want to be a leader? You must be mad. And lots of leaders are! So top tip No. 1 is:

Be Potty for Power!

Here are a few examples of how to be a mad leader.

King Herod the Great (ruled 37 BC–4 BC)

Herod loved Miriam. He wanted to marry her, even though he was already married. (Little things like that don't bother horrors like Herod.)

Miriam hated hideous Herod as soon as she met him, and that doesn't help.

Herod found a funny way to woo Miriam.

Of course it was this King Herod who heard from the Three Wise Men that Jesus was born to be King of the Jews.

Just to be on the safe side, Herod had all the baby boys massacred – but Jesus escaped.

Jesus was lucky – he had a bit of help from an angel of the Lord. The angel decided *not* to help the hundreds of other murdered kids.

As for Herod, he died soon after. As a writer said:

King Charles VI of France (1368–1422)

In April 1392, Charles suffered from a strange illness which made his nails fall out.[2]

As he led his knights through some woods a wild man ran out.

2 This can be very serious if your garden shed catches it.

The little army rode on. It would take more than a wild man to put them off.

Suddenly a young servant dropped a lance. Charles went barmy.

He lost it. He rode around, swishing his sword – and swished four of his knights to death.

From that day on Charles was mentally ill – but it didn't stop him from ruling France.

His doctors came up with a cure: they drilled holes in his skull. Ouch!

Charles felt better for a while.

> *Horrible Histories* warning: Do *not* try this at school – not even if your history teacher goes mad and starts swishing pupils with a stick of chalk.

Then Charles lost his mind again. He believed that:

He ran from room to room crying that his enemies were chasing him. He smashed furniture and piddled in his pants.

Then he had a strange idea.

Charles had iron rods put in his clothes to stop his legs from breaking. He gave up shaving or washing or changing his clothes. He was crawling with lice.

Then his doctors came up with a new cure. They thought, if it was a shock that drove Charles mad, then another shock might drive him back to normal!

Here's how Charles's doctors went about it:

Some people read things in *Horrible Histories* books and say, 'This is so daft it *cannot* be true.' This is one of those stories. Too daft to be true. But, not only is this daft story true, but they reckon it *worked*! Try it on your potty history teacher if you don't believe it.

13

Princess Juana of Castile (1479–1555)

Princess Juana (or Joanna) of Castile in Spain is usually known as 'Juana the Mad'.

JUANA THE MAD

But maybe she wasn't so mad after all.

JUANA THE NOT-VERY-MAD-AFTER-ALL.

When she was a child she was moody and shy. When she grew up she fell madly in love with her husband, Philip the Handsome. But she was also madly jealous of him. Jealousy can drive you to do some crazy things. And Juana was a very jealous woman.

Imagine the scene in Flanders when Philip arrived. If a servant had written a letter home it might have looked like this:

Dear Mum,

It's never boring here, is it? That handsome Philip the Handsome arrived home with his bride.

And, boy, is he handsome. What a hunk! Well, his hair's a bit long, and so is his nose, but all the women love him. And he loves them. He flirts with all the ladies at the court. And, Mum, he even tried flirting with me!

'Hello, beautiful', he says when I serve him some wine. I says, 'less of that, you cheeky man. You're married to Juana!' And he says, 'But my wife's not here, is she?'

No, but she is in the next room. And boy is she the jealous sort! You see, back where she comes from, they are very polite. There's none of that 'Hello beautiful' stuff in Spain. Juana goes stomping around asking questions and bullying the servants. Of course we say nothing about what Philip's been up to. Then she comes up to me and she says, 'Who is my husband's girlfriend?' And I say 'I don't know', and she says, 'Yes you do. Tell me!' And I say, 'I will never betray Lady Anne.' And she says, 'Lady Anne, is it?' And I say 'I never told you that!' And she says, 'Thanks very much!'

15

Anyway, Juana goes barging into the garden where all the ladies is chatting and doing needlework and she says, 'Where is Lady Anne?' Lady Anne looks at jealous Juana and she says, 'Can I help?' and Juana says, 'You can keep your mittens off my husband for a start.'

Anne jumps up all blushing and flustered ~ she knows she's guilty ~ even though none of us would split on her. Anyway she has this letter in her hand and you just know it's a love letter from Phil the Handsome. She tries to hide it behind her back but Juana jumps at her like a cat and snatches it. Lady Anne snatches it back, crumples it into a ball and stuffs it in her mouth. As true as I'm sitting here. She swallows it ~ ink and all. (I think she may have spat out a bit of the sealing wax though.) Well, that drives Juana round the bend. She grabs a pair of scissors from a table and starts hacking at Anne's hair. What a mess! Now Lady Anne starts fighting back ~ you can't blame her.

So Juana takes the scissors and stabs her in the face. Blood everywhere and you should hear the screams!

'Cut her hair off!' Juana orders the servants. 'Cut it all off!' Well we have to obey a princess, don't we? Anyway, I never liked that Lady Anne, stuck-up little snob, no better than she should be. Not that I'd ever give her away, of course. So I help the others hold her down and chop off her hair. I even had a little chop myself. Philip is furious. Handsome, but furious. He comes in and smacks Juana in the face. She doesn't like that, I can tell you. Now he's locked Juana in her bedroom. Even down here in the servants' rooms we can hear her screaming and hammering to get out. We've got a new name for her now: 'Juana the Terror'. Better than Anne the Bald, I suppose. It serves her right. Snobby cow.

I can't sleep for all the screaming. Still, like I said, it's never boring around here.

your loving daughter

Maria
xxx

17

Juana had made herself ill with jealousy. Just after the scissor attack her mother died and Juana returned to Castile as Queen of Spain.

That gave Philip an idea.

So, of course, foul Philip went around making a note of all the daft things she did! Just when he was about to have her locked away, he did something that made her really, *really* mad.

He dropped down dead.

Juana was a bit upset – to say the least.

She cuddled the corpse for a few days before she let them put it in a coffin. What made it worse was that she had been cuddling a corpse that had its heart cut out – Phil's heart was sent back to Flanders for burial. Five weeks later, Juana got the idea that his body had been stolen, so she had the coffin opened up again. She kissed Phil's feet and had to be dragged away. She took the coffin with her wherever she travelled and after a year she had it opened again. (By this time the body was pretty mouldy, as you can probably imagine.)

Her enemies said Juana was potty and that she opened the coffin every day – it was a lie, but the Spanish lords locked her away and gave her throne to her son. From her prison she looked out on the grave of Philip Big-nose. She stayed there for 46 years.

You'd be mad if someone did that to you.

Maybe she is not Juana the Mad. More like Juana the Sad.

Tsar Peter III of Russia (1728–1762)

Peter liked to play with his toy soldiers under the bedclothes every night. He had tiny forts and cannon under there. Cute, eh?

He also made all the sounds of the cannon exploding. Pow! Pow!

But at the same time he had about a dozen spaniel dogs on the bed.

You have to agree, that would be bad behaviour for a ten-year-old boy; except Peter wasn't a ten-year-old boy – he was 34 years old and married to Catherine.

People in those days had a potty under the bed – Catherine had a potty Peter *in* her bed.

She was soon fed up, sharing that bed with toy soldiers, dogs and Peter going, 'Pow! Pow! Pow!'

Catherine had Peter strangled.

Pow!

She blamed his death on piles – a sore bottom.

Ow!

19

King George III of Britain (1738–1820)

Poor old George. He is remembered for one thing – being mad.

In 1788 he fell ill. The first sign of his madness was that he talked non-stop for hours. Sound familiar?

The cures were cruel. George's doctor put hot cups on his skin – as they cooled they sucked out his blood.

It didn't work.

So the palace sent for a mad doctor. He forced George to behave – the King was tied down till he calmed down.

The doctors also fed him medicines. George didn't get any better.

Why not?

Because George III was not mad!

Nowadays doctors say George probably had an illness called porphyria. His medicines had some of the poison arsenic in them. And what makes porphyria *worse*, not better?

Arsenic.

In fact, arsenic in George's wig powder probably made his porphyria start, and his doctors' medicine made it go on and on.

Princess Alexandra of Bavaria (1826–1875)

This Princess shut herself away from the world because she was so upset. What upset her?

Alexandra was sure she had once swallowed a grand piano.

Lots of us swallow grand pianos, of course, but Alex was upset because this one was made of *glass*.

Crazy Carlotta of Spain (1840–1927)

Empress Carlotta was sure everyone was trying to poison her. She was almost starving because she was sure eating any of the food prepared for her would mean certain death.

Carlotta went to visit a convent and passed through the kitchen. A nun offered her some meat stew.

Carlotta was locked away in a mental hospital. Her husband, Emperor Maximilian, was fighting a war against the Mexicans at the time. He was so upset by Carlotta's madness that he gave up the battle.

Max was taken to a hill near Quer'taro to be shot. He gave every man in the firing squad a gold piece, and said:

It did him no good. The first shots didn't kill him – they just smashed his face.

The soldiers had to load their rifles and try again. The second time they managed to kill him.

Bits of his corpse were sold off to people who wanted to remember him.

Bet he was angry. Mad Carlotta then Mad Max.

King Otto of Bavaria (1848–1913)
Otto was sure he was going mad.

He was.

He believed the best way to *stop* himself going mad was to shoot a peasant every day.

He started by taking pot-shots at the workers in the Royal Gardens.

He missed.

But then he started to get better with his aim. So his ministers came up with a clever plan – they would load the King's pistol with blanks. The peasants then had to play dead when they heard the shot.

ROTTEN RULES

Rotten rulers can make up some pretty rotten rules. Could *you* have lived in the days of these lousy leaders?

The Empress Symiamira told the Romans who could ride in a chariot and who had to ride in an ox cart. (Posh people in chariots, of course.)

She told women who could have sandals covered in jewels and who had to have leather sandals. (Posh people with the jewels – you guessed it.)

Other rulers have had odd ideas about crime and punishments. Can you match the punishment to the crime? If you can't then your punishment will be to eat your PE teacher's trainers.

CRIME
1, TAKING A DAY OFF WORK WITHOUT ASKING.
2, REFUSING TO HAVE A HAIRCUT.
3, LAUGHING.
4, WEARING A ROUND HAT.
5, HAVING A WAIST BIGGER THAN 33cm.
6, SAYING THE WORD 'BOMB'.
7, CHATTING.
8, NOT PAYING TAXES.
9, WHISPERING.
10, WEARING GLASSES.

PUNISHMENT
a, BANISHED.
b, KILLED.
c, SACKED.
d, HANGED.
e, BEHEADED.
f, BEATEN UP.
g, STABBED.
h, CHOPPED INTO PIECES.
i, CLUBBED TO DEATH.
j, LOSE YOUR MARKET STALL.

Answers:
1h)
King Gustavus Vasa of Sweden (1496–1560)
Gustavus had a goldsmith who worked for him. One day the goldsmith took a day off without asking Gustavus – a bit like you taking the day off school without asking your teacher. You might have got a detention. Gustavus had his goldsmith chopped into pieces. Gustavus was a bad-tempered vicious Viking. He once tore his daughter's hair out by the roots. And his swearing was terrible. He probably swore as he tore!

IT JUST CAME OFF IN MY HAND. OH, BUMS!

2e)
Emperor Li Yuan Ho
Li Yuan Ho was a Tibetan chief. In 1038 he said,

I AM EMPEROR! GET YOUR HAIR CUT!

Li wanted his men to look different from the other Chinese, so he ordered them to shave their heads except for a fringe at the front. They had three days to comply, after which they would be executed. Sort of chop or be chopped.

3b)
Emperor Caligula of Rome (AD 12–41)
This Roman Emperor was so upset by the death of his sister he said that no one must laugh or take a bath. The punishment was death. What if you did the laugh without the bath? Then at least you died laughing – a bit smelly, but laughing.

4f)
Tsar Paul I of Russia (1754–1801)

This tsad tsar was terrified of a revolution throwing him out on the tseat of his pants. The French had just done it to their king and the French wore *round* hats. Tso what did Tsar Paul do?

That's right – he banned round hats. People were supposed to wear three-cornered hats.

Soldiers went round ripping round hats off round heads and beating the wearers.

If you were a lucky Russian you would be born with a three-cornered head, of course.

Wearing French collars or waistcoats were also crimes that could get you locked up.

5a)

Queen Isabeau of Bavaria (c.1371–1435)

Isabeau married Charles VI of France and decided she wanted all her ladies-in-waiting to have narrow waists. She made a rule that said their waists must measure between 26 and 33 cm.

Any lady who measured more was sent away. Some women starved themselves half to death to obey this foolish rule.

Yet, as she grew older, Isabeau grew so fat that she had to be pushed around in a wheelchair.

When her husband Charles went mad, Isabeau found herself a new boyfriend. Unfortunately Charles became sane again for a while and found out about the boyfriend. The boyfriend was tortured, strangled, tied in a leather sack and thrown into the River Seine.

Fat Isabeau was spared. Maybe they couldn't find a sack big enough.

6c)
Sultan Abdul Hamid II of Turkey (1842–1918)
The Sultan of Turkey was chicken.

He was terrified that someone would kill him.

He…

• was afraid his clothes would be poisoned, so he had clothes testers to put them on before he got dressed
• wore a vest of chain mail
• wore a fez hat with steel inside
• drank milk from his own cow which he milked himself

• carried a gun everywhere (and shot dead a gardener by accident. He also shot a playful daughter who crept up behind him for a surprise. The hole he shot between her eyes was a bigger surprise.)
• kept two pistols by the side of the bath
• had booby-trapped cupboards that could be opened at the touch of a button and shoot a visitor
• carried one of his children on his knee when he went out in his bullet-proof coach – not because he wanted to give the child a ride, but because he wanted the child as a human shield.

Abdul even banned the word 'bomb' in Turkey – he didn't want people talking about bomb plots to kill him.

The Sultan's chief cook made a delicious dessert – a hollow ball of ice-cream filled with fruit and custard. The name of this tasty treat is French. It is called *bombe glacé*. When the Sultan saw the word 'bombe' he freaked. The chef was sacked.

But it all seemed to work. He died peacefully in his bed aged 77 – not many rotten rulers managed that.

7j)
King Frederick William I of Prussia (1688–1740)

In Prussia women looked after the stalls in the markets. When they were not busy they liked to sit and chat. Fred banned that – he said women must keep themselves occupied by knitting stockings. No chatting or you lose your stall – lose your stall and you starve.

Frederick William was cruel to the master of the Prussian Science School, Jakob Paul Gundling. The poor man had the job of reading the newspapers to the King. The King and his friends tormented him – once they set him on fire. Jakob eventually drank himself to death. Foul Fred had the master buried in a beer barrel.

8d)
Nadir Shah of Persia (1688–1747)

Nasty Nadir wanted huge armies so he could go around bashing his neighbours. But armies cost money and the money came from taxes on the people. Anyone who could not pay was executed.

Nadir thought his own son, Reza Quli Mirza, was plotting against him.

Did Nadir give him a slap round the ear and tell him to behave? No.

Did he lock him in his room till he said 'Sorry'? No. He had him blinded.

But some of his lords knew what Nadir had done – so Nadir had the lords executed to keep them quiet.

Nadir enjoyed going on journeys round his country. But wherever he stopped to rest he had people tortured and put to death.

Nasty Nadir had towers built from the skulls of his victims.

In March 1747 he crossed the pitiless Dasht-i-Lut desert, where many of his men died from hunger and thirst.

A group of his own tribe did not want to be next. As one chief said:

WE DECIDED TO HAVE HIM FOR BREAKFAST BEFORE HE HAD US FOR SUPPER

They attacked him in his sleep. He still managed to kill two attackers before they lopped off his head.

Nadir lost his nut.

9g)

King Eric XIV of Sweden (1533–1577)

Eric was sure people were out to get him. So he attacked anyone in his palace who whispered behind his back.

A sudden movement? It could get you sliced like a piece of bacon.

A cough at the wrong time? It could get you pierced like a pudding.

Eric even went around stabbing servants who dressed too well – if they looked too smart (he said) then they must be trying to chat up the ladies in his court. A quick carving would put a stop to that.

He had the top Swedes thrown into prison – then he murdered one in his cell and told the guards to kill all the others.

As he rode from the prison Eric met his dear old teacher Dionysius. He stabbed the old teacher to death. In the end Eric's brother John III took his throne and had Eric put in jail. John wrote a letter to the jailer:

> *If anyone tries to set my brother free then poison him.*

Eric was poisoned.

SEE! I TOLD YOU THEY WERE OUT TO GET ME!

10i)
Pol Pot, Cambodian ruler (ruled 1975–1979)
About 1.7 million Cambodians died of starvation, disease, overwork and execution during Pol Pot's rule.
He wanted Cambodia to go back to a sort of Middle Ages when life was simple and peasants were pure.

In those simple days few people could read, so no one needed glasses. If Pol Pot's bully boys (the Khmer Rouge) caught you wearing glasses you'd be beaten to death – often with a shovel.

Pol Pot used to be a teacher. His 'rules' were a bit tougher than your school rules. Apart from wearing glasses, you could be executed for:
• not working hard enough
• complaining
• stealing food
• wearing jewellery
• crying for a dead friend
• praying

When Pol Pot died he was buried in the mountains of Anlong Veng. What did the Cambodians do with this monster's grave site in June 2004?

They turned it into a theme park for tourists.

You can go and see the place where landmines were made; or trek to the jungle where Pol Pot was cremated on a pile of burning tyres.

LOATHSOME LEADER: EMPEROR ELAGABALUS OF ROME (AD 203-222)

Little Varius was pushed on to the throne by his mother when he was just 14 years old.

Mummy made him the High Priest of Elagabalus, the sun god. That meant he sacrificed hundreds of sheep and cattle in the temple and then poured rich wine over the blood-dripping bodies.

Yummy.

After a while the sad lad really began to believe he *was* the sun god and changed his name to Elagabalus.

The young god invited friends to dinner and made them wrestle with lions and eat live parrots.

His enemies were tied to a wall so he could stab them with red-hot pokers. Strips of skin were torn off them and they were dipped in salty water.

You wouldn't believe the things he did. Or would you?

Lousy life

Here are 15 foul facts about Elagabalus' life. *One* is a lie – but which one?

1 He acted in plays and played the part of the goddess Venus – with no clothes on.
2 He liked to dress like a woman. He used to paint his eyes and rouge his cheeks, and was shaved all over his body.
3 He started to sacrifice children in the temples but he only killed

children who still had *two* parents so there was twice the misery.

4 He examined the guts of sacrificed children so he could see into the future and displayed the guts in golden bowls.

5 He often feasted on a dish of peas mixed with nuggets of gold.

6 He served his guests joke food made of wax or stone and they had to pretend to enjoy it.

7 He gave away cattle, asses and slaves as presents to the people.

8 He had a naval show where the ships floated on a lake of wine.

9 He slipped bears and wild cats into guests' bedrooms while they slept.

10 He ordered a slave to collect 500 kilos of spiders' webs – the slave failed and was eaten alive by starving rats.

11 He played games where prizes were gold or lettuce leaves, diamonds or scorpions.

12 He had a trick ceiling in his dining room. It opened up to flood the room with rose and violet petals, but these suffocated the guests.

13 He rewarded a dancing girl by hanging a dead dog around her neck.

14 He gathered crowds to watch a show then scattered poisoned snakes among them so he could watch people being bitten or trampled in panic.

15 He had great feasts where everyone was forced to eat school dinners.

Answer: **Number 15 is the fake. It was not really that difficult. If you got one wrong then you deserve an invite to an Elagabalus party.**

Ela-gobble-ups

A cockerel has a red 'comb' on the top of its head. This was sliced off while the cockerel was still alive, cooked, and served to the Emperor.

The crafty cooks told him:

His guests were shocked. Nor were they too happy watching the Emperor chewing away at cooked camel heels.

The Emperor also ate flamingo, partridge and thrush brains. 600 flamingo heads were served at one party. Guests had to scoop out the brains with a golden spoon. None of these things made Elagabalus any brainier. He also ate the heads of parrots, pheasants and peacocks. (You'll notice he never ate the heads of toucans or pelicans because the bill was too much.)

Elagabalus fed his dogs on goose liver and his horses on old grapes.

His pet lions enjoyed sow udders.

Elagabalus's army was fed up with him so the soldiers decided to kill him.

He tried to run away and locked himself in the toilet. That's where they killed him.

They poured boiling, molten gold into his eyes.

They grabbed his corpse with meat hooks and lugged it through the dusty streets. Then they tried stuffing the dead Emperor down a sewer so he'd be washed into the river. But the body got stuck.

The killers hauled him out, and dragged him round the chariot race-track. Finally they took him to the nearest bridge and threw him into the River Tiber.

The Emperor's unpopular mother was thrown in with him.

HAPPY FAMILIES

Rulers have always had enemies who wanted to kill them. Often, their worst enemies were members of their own family.

Brutal brothers, slaying sisters, savage sons and murderous mothers, deadly dads and – oh, finish it yourself; you get the idea.

Here are a few foul family facts.

Julius Caesar of Austria (1585–1609)
Rudolf was *not* a red-nosed reindeer, he was King of Austria.

Old Rudolf had some very odd children, but the oddest of all was the one called Julius Caesar. Do not mix him up with the Roman Julius Caesar.

Rudolf had to lock young Julius away for a while because the boy had battered one of his servants half to death.

What do you think he did when he was set free?

Yes, you could say that Caesar seized her. (Or maybe you'd rather not say that.)

The girl was ordered to return to Julius. Her father refused to let her go back to jabbing Jules so the father was thrown into jail. The girl went back.

Sultan Mustafa of Turkey (1592–1639)

Mustafa wasn't very bright. When his big brother Ahmed became ruler in 1603, he shut Mustafa up in a building with no windows.

Here is a rare *Horrible Histories* picture of Mustafa inside the building at night.

Here is an even rarer *Horrible Histories* picture of Mustafa inside the building one day.

The building was called the Cage.[3]

But then Ahmed died, so Mustafa was allowed out to become Sultan.

He was 26, but he still had the mind of a child, so the army put him back in the Cage. This time, Mustafa refused to come out. At least he had a couple of girlfriends in the Cage with him.

(Sorry – we have no picture of Mustafa in the Cage with his girlfriends and here it is.)

The Turkish army made a hole in the roof and hauled Mustafa out to be Sultan *again* when the next ruler died.

But Mad Mustafa was still mad. He gave the job of High Priest to a donkey driver that he had taken a shine to.

He was shut up in the Cage one last time (after the roof had been mended) and he stayed there for another 16 years, until he died at the age of 47.

3 Please note − these pictures have never been published before and are priceless. All rights reserved. That means they must not be copied unless you send the author a million pounds (though he might settle for £5 and a bag of jelly babies if you ask him nicely).

Prince Frederick of Great Britain (1707–1751)

This Prince was known as 'Poor Fred' because his family hated him so much.

His father, George II, said:

He is the greatest villain that ever was born. I wish the ground would open at this moment and sink the monster to the lowest hole in Hell.

Fred's mum, Caroline of Ansbach, was no better. She said:

He is the greatest ass, and the greatest beast, in the whole world. At least when I die I will never have to see him again.

And sister Caroline was the most charming of all. She said:

I wish that he may die. Then we may all go about with smiling faces and glad hearts.

YOU DON'T LIKE ME THEN?

Frederick never became King Fred I of Great Britain because he died after a nasty accident – he was hit in the head by a cricket ball. (Some reports say it was a tennis ball, but we do know Fred was keen on cricket.)

Not everyone hated Fred. When he died some sympathetic person wrote a poem saying it would have been better if the rest of his family had died instead:

Here lies poor
Fred who was alive
and is dead,
Had it been his father,
I had much rather,
Had it been his sister
nobody would have
missed her,
Had it been his brother
still better than another,
Had it been the whole
generation so much better
for the nation,
But since it is Fred who
was alive and is dead,
There is no
more to be said

None of his family went to the funeral.
Poor Fred.

Prince Sado of Korea (1735–1762)

If Sado was mad-o it was because of his dad-o.

Young Sado was very ill when he was just ten and he started having nightmares. He thought he could see the terrifying god of Thunder.

But his dad, King Yongjo, was even more terrifying.

When the King had a nasty job to do he would often make young Sado do it instead of him.

As Prince Sado grew older, he became more cruel and violent. He:
• beat his servants
• murdered a guard then stuck the dead man's head on a pole and showed it to the ladies in the palace
• started killing maids

Sado said:

Doctors came to treat him. He killed them.

The busiest people in the palace were the ones who carried the corpses away – every day.

On 4 July 1762, Prince Sado was called to see his father, the King.

The King had a wooden chest brought in. Sado was locked in the chest and left to starve. After eight days the chest was opened and Sado was found dead.

That's a bit tough on Sado – but then, he had been a vicious murderer.

A worse fate was in store for his servants, workmen and fortune-tellers. They were all put to death, too – even though they'd done nothing wrong.

President Francisco Lopez of Paraguay (1826–1870)

Francisco was fatter than a barrel of lard, and he was a bigger bully than Desperate Dan.

He picked on everyone, but he saved his nastiest bit of cruelty for his own family.

One day his frail old mother told him:

47

Francisco Lopez also told the church leaders that he should be made a saint. Twenty-three bishops disagreed.

They were shot.

Marriages made in hell

If you want to be a film star it helps to be handsome. But if you want to be a leader it doesn't seem to matter what you look like – in fact the uglier the better!

Empress Josepha of Austria (1683–1745)

Poor Josepha was spotty. So spotty, her husband, Joseph, couldn't bear to touch her. He said:

I just wish I could put one fingertip on one part of her body that isn't covered in boils.

They never had children.

Queen Barbara of Portugal (1711–1758)

King Ferdinand of Spain married Barbara of Portugal because his family said he had to – they said it would make Spain and Portugal friends.

He seemed to love her chubby little face, scarred from smallpox, and her body as fat as a water-filled balloon.

For some reason the Spanish people never liked her though. She was sure they were plotting to kill her.

They didn't need to. Barbara got a cough and grew thin and died.

As they say in Wolverhampton-on-Sea:

Duke Philippe of Orleans (1640–1701)

Philippe was told he had to marry Princess Elizabeth of Bavaria in 1671. She was at least 45 cm taller than him, and he was terrified of her.

Phil and Liz slept in the same bed, but the poor Princess was forced to sleep on the edge. Most nights she ended up crashing to the floor.

King Frederick William II of Prussia (1744–1797)
Fred was told by his father, 'You must marry Princess Elizabeth.'

Fred argued, 'But she is ugly *and* very smelly.'

The Prince was desperate. He promised:

IF YOU FORCE ME TO MARRY HER, I'LL KILL MYSELF!

DON'T BOTHER. IF YOU REFUSE TO MARRY HER I'LL HAVE YOU KILLED!

Fred and Liz married in 1765 – and he didn't kill himself. But he did divorce her as soon as he could – in 1769.

Princess Maria Christina of Habsburg (1574–1621)
In 1595 Zsigmond married Princess Maria Christina of Habsburg. He said:

SHE IS HIDEOUS! I WAKE AT NIGHT AND FIND HER BY MY SIDE. I CAN'T HELP SCREAMING IN TERROR!

Howzat?
Here are some odd facts about rotten rulers. They are true. But can you explain them?

Here's an example: Britain used to rule America but lost it because of a cricket ball. How is that? Or 'Howzat!' as they say in cricket games?

The answer is:
• Prince Frederick of Great Britain was killed by a cricket ball, so…
• his son George III became the next king and George was mentally ill, so…
• a little trouble in America became a war and Britain lost, so …
• if that cricket ball had missed Fred's head then America could still be British

See? Try these Howzats on your poor parent, or torment a teacher.

1 In 1283 the Welsh ruler Dafydd ap Gruffydd (c.1235–1283) had his heart ripped out and burned. Dafydd then blinded his executioner. Howzat?

2 Prince Sado of Korea ran away from his angry father and jumped into a deep well to hide. Sado didn't get wet and he didn't drown. Howzat?

3 Prince Christian VII of Denmark (1749–1808) was born long before nightclubs were invented, yet he used to love to go out clubbing with his friends. Howzat?

4 Frederick II of Prussia (1712–1786) was really Frederick IV. His dad was Frederick I. Howzat?

5 Dogs have 16 toes, but in the days of William the Conqueror most dogs had just four toes. Howzat?

6 Roman Emperor Caligula went to a wedding where the bride got married – but not to the bridegroom. Howzat?

7 Carlos II of Spain (1661–1700) had a dead pigeon on his head and died. Howzat?

8 King Abbad el Motaddid, King of the Moors (in Spain)

cut off the heads of his enemies. He kept the skulls full of life. Howzat?

9 The Aztec Emperor Montezuma used to talk to piles of poo, played with piles of poo and even had piles of poo on his knee. Howzat?

10 During the AD 900s, the Grand Vizier of Persia took 117,000 books wherever he went. They were carried by camels. The Vizier always knew where to find a book. Howzat?

Answers:

1) King Edward I of England ordered that Dafydd be torn apart by horses. The executioner then had to cut open the body, rip out the heart, and burn it on a coal fire. The executioner cut out the heart, which was still beating, and threw it on the fire. The heart exploded and jumped from the fire with one of the coals stuck to it. The heart hit the executioner in the face and the coal blinded him.

2) The well was frozen over. The palace guards soon rescued him.

3) Christian used to skulk along the dark streets of Copenhagen with a gang of friends. They were armed with spiked clubs – the sort that knights used in the Middle Ages. He used this to club unlucky people in the street.

4) A baby named Frederick came Second, but he had a crown jammed on his head as he was christened. It crushed his skull. Another baby named Frederick came Third. The palace fired cannon from the roofs to let the world know. Sadly the cannon were too near the baby and the shock killed him. Along came a Fourth Frederick who lived to be crowned Frederick the Second – even though he was fourth.

See?

5) King William ordered that any hunting dogs that did not belong to him had to have three toes cut off each foot. This would slow them down while trying to catch deer and hares. William's dogs would then get all the best game.

6) Caligula liked the bride, Livia Orestilla, so much that he snatched her from the bridegroom and married her himself. He divorced her a few days later. She was lucky! Caligula had a nasty habit of kissing the necks of his wives and saying, 'This lovely neck can be chopped as soon as I say so.'

7) Carlos was dying. One of the treatments doctors used in those days was to kill a pigeon and place its corpse on the King's head. It didn't work. They also put the steaming guts of dead animals on his stomach to keep him warm. Carlos ended up as dead as the animals, of course – only smellier and slimier.

8) King Abbad used the skulls as flower-pots.

9) Montezuma had a nephew called Cuitlahac, which means 'Piles of poo'.

10) The camels were trained to walk in alphabetical order.

FOOD FIT FOR A KING

Rulers usually eat well.

Queen Victoria of Great Britain (1819–1901)

While the poor were fighting over bones or chewing on scraps of stale bread, Queen Victoria was living a very rich life. The Queen never seemed to realize that her poor subjects were starving. In 1839 she went to a

NO WE DON'T. WE ARE BAD EATERS – WICKED IN FACT. WE EAT FAR TOO MUCH WHILE OTHERS STARVE. IT'S ALL PART OF OUR JOB

banquet with the Lord Mayor of London. Compare that banquet of *two and a half hours* with the food of Robert Crick's family. Robert was a Suffolk farm worker, and his banquet had to last the whole family a whole *week*.

Robert Crick's family –
Number at the table: 7
Food:
Bread – Sugar – Butter – Salt –
Potatoes – Cheese – Tea.
Cost: 55p
1p a day each.

Victoria's friends

Number at the table: 570

Food:

220 SERVING BOWLS OF SOUP
45 DISHES OF SHELLFISH
2 SIDES OF BEEF
10 SIRLOINS, RUMPS AND RIBS OF BEEF
50 BOILED TURKEYS WITH OYSTERS
80 PHEASANTS
60 PIGEON PIES
45 DECORATED HAMS
140 JELLIES
200 ICE CREAMS
40 DISHES OF TARTS
100 PINEAPPLES
VARIOUS OTHER DISHES
CHAMPAGNES AND WINES

Cost: £8172.25
£14.33 a day each.

And they said Henry VIII was a great greedy glutton!

Victoria's doctor had the pleasure of seeing her without her clothes on. He said:

> *She is more like a barrel than anything else.*

King George I of Great Britain (1660–1727)

Gorging George was seasick. He tried to cure it by pigging out on melons. That probably brought on the stroke that killed him.

> I'M DYING FOR A MELON

> HE WILL BE!

King George II of Great Britain (1683–1760)

George had a disgusting habit of making very loud botty-burps. One evening he went off to the toilet and his servant heard a huge explosion from the King's backside.

When the servant opened the door he found George dead. He'd fallen off the toilet and smashed his head into a cabinet.

Maybe he had blown himself off the toilet! If the cabinet hadn't been there to stop him, he might have been the first ruler in space.

King George III of Great Britain (1738–1820)

George III was mentally ill when he started burying beef steaks in the palace gardens. He thought they would grow into beef-steak trees.

King Louis XVI of France (1754–1793)

Lou had a huge appetite. What did his servants call him?

a) Lardy Lou
b) King Kong
c) The Fat Pig

Answer: **c)** The French Revolution cured his bad habit and Louis lost a couple of kilos of ugly flesh in a few moments. The guillotine sliced off his head. The Fat Pig's neck was so thick it took two chops to get through.

Emperor Vitellius of Rome (ruled AD 15–16)

This Roman was about the greediest man who ever lived. His nickname was 'The Glutton'.

He never stopped eating. When a sacrifice was cooked for the gods, Vitellius ate it all.

Then he seemed to be going for a world record.

He had a single dish made – the size of a large room. He ordered the dish to be filled with the rarest foods around.

These included:
• pike livers
• pheasant brains
• peacock brains
• flamingo tongues
• eel spleens

These were all to be covered in tasty sauces.

How did piggy Vitellius kill his own mother?

a) He fed her till she burst.
b) He starved her.
c) He fed her a poisoned peacock pie.

Answer: **b)** Well, at least he didn't eat her.

You will be pleased to know he died a really suitable death: he was scoffing a crow for dinner and choked on its beak.

STONE THE CROWS!

Sultan Abdul Aziz of Turkey (1830–1876)

Sultan Aziz was fat. He weighed around 105 kilos and needed a bed about 2.5 metres wide.

How did he get so fat? From eating eggs – boiled or fried.

The bits that he didn't eat he used to pelt at his servants. This explains the famous Turkish saying:

He ate off golden plates encrusted with rubies. This must have made his fried eggs taste better. (Try eating your school dinner's lumpy mashed potato off gold plates and see for yourself.)

His hobby was chasing chickens round the royal palace. When he caught one he didn't eat it – he put a medal round its neck.

He had 900 wives. They probably egged him on, crying 'Come on, your egg-celency!'

Fat Abdul was thrown off his throne and killed himself. How?

a) He stuffed a hard-boiled egg down his throat till he choked.

b) He cut his throat with a pair of scissors.

c) He escaped from his palace window and jumped into the swimming pool below – but he was so fat he plunged to the bottom and cracked his skull. (He also damaged the tiles at the bottom of the pool.)

> *Answer:* **b)** He asked for a pair of scissors so he could trim his beard. After he'd trimmed his beard, he just sort of kept going with the scissors.

4 All right, it isn't a famous Turkish saying. In fact no one is daft enough to say such a bad joke ... you won't even see it in a *Horrible Histories* book.

Did you know…?

The Holy Roman Emperor Frederick II (1194–1250) was interested in how our bodies digest food. So he found out. He invited guests to dinner. Then he killed them and cut them open.

Nice man!

Emperor Shih Hu of China (ruled AD 334–349)

Lots of men like to take a woman friend out for dinner.

Emperor Shih Hu liked to have a girlfriend for dinner. The difference with Shih Hu's girlfriend is that she *was* the dinner.

At a big feast he would have a girl beheaded and cooked. Then her head was passed around the table. He wanted to show his guests how lucky they were. He was saying:

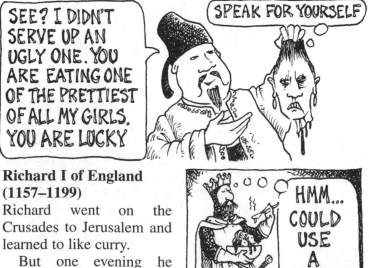

SEE? I DIDN'T SERVE UP AN UGLY ONE. YOU ARE EATING ONE OF THE PRETTIEST OF ALL MY GIRLS. YOU ARE LUCKY

SPEAK FOR YOURSELF

Richard I of England (1157–1199)

Richard went on the Crusades to Jerusalem and learned to like curry.

But one evening he enjoyed a particularly spicy and spiteful dish. He had the head of a Saracen enemy cut off and curried. Then he ate it.

HMM… COULD USE A POPPADOM

Richard was nicknamed 'Lionheart' and is supposed to be an English hero – but they don't tell you about his terrible tastes in school.

Or in skull.

Sioux Indian Chief Rain-in-the-face (1876)

He was one of the native Amerians who fought at The battle of the Little Big Horn. This battle is better known as "Custer's Last Stand".

The US cavalry were massacred. It was said that Chief Rain-in-the-face ripped out the heart of the US soldier Tom Custer and ate it.

The Chief himself said, "No. After the battle we young men were chasing horses all over the prairie. The old men and women robbed the bodies, and if any damage was done to the corpses, it was done by the old men."

President Jean-Bédel Bokassa of the Central African Republic (1921–1996)

When Jean-Bédel took over the country he had a huge party for his coronation. He invited all the world leaders.

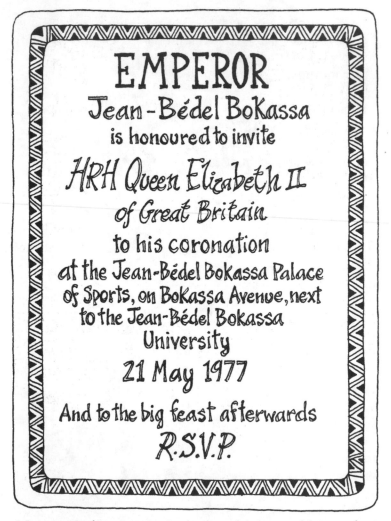

EMPEROR
Jean-Bédel Bokassa
is honoured to invite

HRH Queen Elizabeth II
of Great Britain

to his coronation
at the Jean-Bédel Bokassa Palace
of Sports, on Bokassa Avenue, next
to the Jean-Bédel Bokassa
University

21 May 1977

And to the big feast afterwards

R.S.V.P.

Most countries sent the invitations back or said no – they knew Bokassa was a cruel killer.

But some countries, like Italy and Germany, *did* send ministers to the coronation. Big mistake.

What they didn't know was that a few weeks before, 100 children from Bangui, the capital city of the Central African Republic, had held a protest march.

The children were arrested for not wearing school uniforms.

Then they were murdered.

Then they were cooked and served at the coronation feast.

Four months later Jean-Bédel Bokassa was overthrown and put on trial. He was not executed, but he did spend a few years in jail before he was released.

Deadly drink

1) Alexander the Great (356–323 BC) had boozing competitions. The person who could drink the most wine was the winner (or the winer). In one contest, 35 men died from the alcohol. Alexander's friend Hephaestion died drinking half a gallon (over 2 litres) of wine for breakfast.

LET'S CONQUER THE WORLD!

I'LL DRINK TO THAT

On another occasion Alex became so drunk that he killed three friends with a spear.

But in the end the winner was the booze. Drinking killed Alexander.

2) Queen Elizabeth I of England (1533–1603) had terrible skin – all wrinkled and marked with spots. How did she try to make it better? She drank puppy pee.

How do you get a puppy to pee in a cup? You can't. You just have to wait until it makes a poodle on the floor; soak it up with a cloth, then squeeze the cloth into your cup.

Yummy.

She also made hair cream from apples and puppy fat. Tudor times were terrible for mini-mutts.

3) When Mehmet II of Turkey (1429–1481) found a melon had gone missing he was sure one of 14 servants had stolen it.

Did he send for Sherlock Holmes to solve the mystery of the missing melon? No, he didn't.

Did he check the fruit-bowl for fingerprints? No.

Did he cut open the stomachs of the 14 servants to find it? Yes, he did.

Did he eat the melon afterwards? What do you think?

LOATHSOME LEADER: IVAN IV 'THE TERRIBLE' OF RUSSIA (1530~1584)

In fact he was so – erm – *awesome* that you would be disgusted by his life-story.

So I won't tell you.

What? You still want to read it? Oh, very well.

I'll tell you the story but I'll leave out the gruesome bits. You can fill them in for yourself – then, if you are sick all over your rat pie and chips, you can't blame me.[5]

5 A survey from 2004 showed that 67.8% of *Horrible Histories* readers enjoy rat pie and chips. Only 21.4% like mouse eyeballs on toast.

You want a few clues? Oh, go on then. Here are the missing words (in the wrong order, of course.)

leg, bird, soup, flea, coal, witch, temper, feather, dog, skin, scream, spider, blood, body, eye, hair, jester

Ivan was terrible even when he was a kid. His hobby was torturing animals and he liked throwing a (   ) off the roof of the palace. If he could catch a (   ) he would tear out every (   ) and poke out each (   ) before slitting it open. As for a (   ), he'd pull off each (   ) and watch it spin round, helpless.

As he grew up he had a dreadful (   ) – sometimes, in a rage, he ripped out his (   ) till his head was covered in (   ).

He enjoyed torturing his enemies. Prince Michael Vorotynski was accused of being a (   ) so he was burned alive. Ivan raked the hot (   ) over his struggling (   ). His minister Founilov was dipped in boiling water then cold water over and over till his (   ) peeled off like a grape.

Sometimes Ivan could be funny – like when he ordered citizens to bring him a cartload of (   ) bodies. He also laughed. He laughed as he tipped scalding (   ) over his (   ). When he gave a (   ) Ivan stabbed him to death.

So what can awesome Ivan teach us about ruling?
Quite a lot.

Ivan the Awesome's Cool Rules

① Start young. I was aged three when I came to the throne, and 14 when I had a putrid prince thrown ✳ to the dogs to be torn apart.

② Don't waste time with trials. When I attacked rebel towns I always used to say, 'The people are guilty. I can see it in their faces'. Then I had them executed.

Guilty!

③ Be savage. I don't mess around with quick, painless hangings. I sometimes had ribs torn out of rebels using hot iron pincers. If a woman killed her husband she was buried alive.

④ Terrify the people. I had pots of boiling oil waiting to dip my enemies in. Others were roasted on spits like joints of meat.

5 Children get chopped too. I liked to see a child tied to its mother before both were run through with a single sword. And I often ordered boys to kill their own fathers (before I had the boys killed, of course).

6 Keep going. It's not enough to kill a few hundred. People soon forget. I killed around 50,000. And I left them lying around for the dogs to eat. They remember me.

7 Get a bodyguard. I had a troop called the 'Oprichniki' and were real terrors. They dressed in black and rode black horses. Many were drunks and criminals - all were happy to murder a priest at his altar. Ruthless and loyal.

⑧ Get a wife or two. I had eight. When I grew tired of them I sent the lucky ones to a convent. Unlucky ones like Maria Dolgurukaya were drowned. Nothing worse than a wet wife.

⑨ Get a temper. People fear you if you fly into rages. In one rage I struck my son on the forehead with a spear. He died. Poor boy. But my rages were splendid and I foamed at the mouth like a horse.

⑩ Enjoy yourself. There's no point in all this ruling if you don't enjoy it. I went around the streets of Moscow with a gang of friends and beat up strangers. Old people were the easiest.

Did you know...?
Ivan loved his new church, St Basil's. The men who built it were rewarded – by being blinded. Ivan didn't want them to make anything better.

TOP OF THE TOTS

Rulers were often the children of the previous ruler. So here's a top tip for tots:

Make sure your mum or dad is a ruler and you can have a quick trip to the throne.

This is rather like playing Snakes and Ladders. You can zip up the ladders, but you have to watch out for the snakes!

**Tartar conqueror
Tamerlane the Great
(1336–1405)**

Tamerlane's family was related to the mighty Genghis Khan – which is a good start in life.

But Tamerlane himself was meant to be a ruthless ruler from the second he was born.

How did his family know? Because baby Tamerlane was born with blood-filled hands. A deadly sign.

Sure enough, his hands were steeped in blood for the rest of his life.

When he invaded India he massacred 100,000 Hindu prisoners in Delhi. Why? Because it was too much trouble to feed them and guard them.

Then he entered the city and killed *another* 100,000!

Think of all those corpses! It would have been easier to feed them than to bury them.

Prince Fritz of Prussia (1712–1786)

Fritz's father, King Frederick William I, decided he wanted his son to grow up tough. So:

• Baby Fritz was woken each morning by the firing of a cannon.

• When he was six he was given his own army of children to lead.

• When he was seven they were given guns.

• Young Fritz was beaten for falling off a horse.

• He was whipped for wearing gloves on a cold day.

71

King Frederick William wrote down orders for Fritz's teachers.

On Sunday Prince Fritz must get out of bed at seven. As soon as he has his slippers on he shall kneel at the bed and say a short prayer to God. He must speak loud enough for his servants to hear. Then he must say the Lord's prayer. Then he must dress and wash himself quickly. He must have his hair combed and powdered.

He must have his breakfast while his hair is being done and be finished in a quarter of an hour, that is, by a quarter past seven.

Frederick William (King)

If you think that's a bit like a prison or a school then that's what Fritz thought, too.

Sometimes his dangerous dad would grab him by the throat and throw him on to the ground. Fritz told his sister:

I AM SO TIRED OF IT ALL I WOULD RATHER BEG FOR BREAD THEN GO ON LIVING LIKE THIS!

Fritz grew up to be Frederick the Great – which just goes to show... something.

Princess Catalina of Spain (1507–1525)

Princess Catalina's dad died before she was born. Her mum (Juana of Spain) was sure that Catalina's baby babble was the dead dad talking through the child!

The only fun the little girl had was looking out of a window. Juana guarded baby Catalina jealously. She made her live and sleep in her own room. She saw no one but her mother and two servants.

It was like a baby prison, and not very healthy. At the age of ten Catalina was still living in a tower with her sad mother. The princess didn't wear silk gowns; she wore a sheepskin jacket.

She didn't eat fine feasts; she shared her mother's bread and cheese. Catalina died at the age of 18.

She was probably happy to go.

73

Princess Kristina of Sweden (1599–1655)

Kristina was the daughter of King Gustavus Adolphus II of Sweden.

Before she was born a fortune teller said:

Kristina was born covered in woolly hair – a fleece – which covered her from head to knees. All you could see was the face, arms and lower legs. The doctors told the smiling king:

Then they discovered it was a girl. No one dared to tell the King. So they just handed the baby to him and let him find out for himself.

He wasn't angry. He just said:

The Queen, Maria Eleonore, was not so happy. She ranted and screamed.

Poor baby Kristina suffered from her mother's hatred. She had lots of accidents as a child – a large plank fell on her cradle and she fell down stairs. Kristina was dropped on a stone floor and crushed her shoulder.

But the nastiest little horror happened when the King died.

Did you know…?

You may think royal princes had a tough childhood. But at least they had a childhood.

In the 1600s, sultans of the Ottoman Empire were worried that their children would grow up and take their thrones. So what did they do with their children?

a) Sent them to live with peasants

b) Killed them

c) Ate them

Answer: **b)** After 1607 the princesses' children were usually killed at birth.

Tsar Ivan VI of Russia (1740–1764)

Now you've met some little leaders you should be able to work out the terrible truth for yourself about someone like Ivan VI. So here are his details with the numbers missing. Just fill in the blanks.

Clues:

The numbers (in the wrong order) are: 2, 2, 4, 5, 13, 20, 22, 23, 27 and 64.

The dates above will also help.

Ivan VI was the great-grandson of simple-minded Ivan ( ) of Russia. So he had no chance.

When he was aged ( ) months he was made Emperor. Ernst Johann Béhren, the Duke of Courland, was the real ruler, though.

Evil Ernst was so unpopular he only lasted ( ) days. Baby Ivan's mother, Anna Leopoldovna, took control.

But baby Ivan only ruled for ( ) months. He and his mum were locked away. This did not prevent Ivan's mum having ( ) more babies. But she died at the age of ( ).

Poor little Ivan was placed under strong guard in an island fortress, Schlüsselburg, for ( ) years. He saw no family and little sunlight. He was dressed in rags and frequently went hungry. His drunken guards often beat him.

Catherine the Great visited Ivan and found he was witless. Then in 17( ) a soldier tried to rescue him. The guards assassinated Ivan. This meant that Catherine had murdered ( ) tsars.

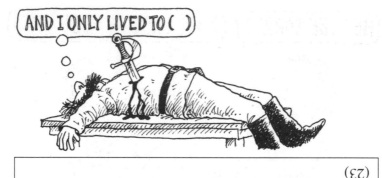

The *Horrible Histories* brainometer says that if you got ten out of ten you probably cheated. If you got four or less you are probably the great-grandchild of a simple-minded tsar.

Don Carlos of Spain (1545–1568)

Little Carlos had brain damage, and that probably made him violent.

If *you* did some of the things he did then you'd be stopped. But Carlos was a ruler so they let him get away with:

- torturing little girls and servants
- going into the palace stables and carving the horses so badly that twenty of them had to be put down
- roasting small animals alive, especially hares
- biting the head off a ring-snake

When he grew up he was no better. He:

- tried to throw a servant out of a palace window
- forced a shoemaker to eat a pair of boots that were badly made

As Don Carlos didn't say:

In 1562 Don Carlos fell down a stairwell in the dark and gashed his head horribly.

It swelled and swelled like a pumpkin and he went blind. The doctors cut holes in his head, but that didn't help. Then some monks brought a precious 'relic' from their monastery – the mummy of a saint who had died 100 years before. The mummy was put in bed with the sick prince – yeuch!

That night Carlos dreamed of the saint and, believe it or not, he started to get better.

Cruel Carlos was such a nuisance that eventually he was locked away in a tower, and there he died.

Some people said his father had him poisoned.

King Erik XIV of Sweden (1533–1577)

Erik's father, Gustavus Vasa, was another deadly dad. When his daughter Cecile made him angry, he grabbed her hair and tore it out by the roots.

Cecile died young (and probably bald). It was said that violent Gustavus had killed her in a rage.

And you thought detention was bad?

Erik was as potty as his pa. Some people must have been glad when they read of his death.

The Swedish Sun

STILL ONLY 20 KRONA

26 February 1577

EXIT ERIK

GET YOUR FREE☆ BAG OF SWEDES! COLLECT THE TOKENS ☆ INSIDE ☆

KRAZY KING KICKS BUCKET

The Palace at Stockholm said today that King Erik is dead. Our crackpot King was as daft as his dad, Gustavus. People of Sweden can whisper again! That's right, Erik was worried about people talking behind his back, so whisperers were whittled down with his sword. Someone who coughed at the wrong moment was accused of plotting – the cough was a signal, he said. And that was just part of his cruel rule.

He started ruling back in 1560 and soon showed his nasty side. Two guards annoyed him so he had them executed. His own brother, John, was thrown in jail for the crime of getting married, and his trusty servants were put to the sword.

Top minister Nils Sture's family was locked up in Uppsala Castle, on charges of treason. On 24 May 1566 Evil Erik said he wanted to visit Nils and forgive him. But the King didn't say a word – just stabbed him to death. Then he ran from the castle, ordering the guards to kill *all* the prisoners.

Of course Erik gave Nils a great funeral.

Now it's Erik's funeral. He was pushed from the palace by brother John and sent to Örbyhus Castle, where he died earlier today.

A spokesman for King John told our reporter that Erik was not poisoned. Our reporter said that poison was found in the body. The spokesman said, 'Er well, I don't know how that got there, I'm sure. Someone must have made a mistake.'

John becomes King John III. The *Swedish Sun* wishes his majesty a long and happy reign. Long live the King! (The new King, that is, not the old one who cannot live long as he's dead.)

81

Erik certainly *was* poisoned. That's little brothers for you. A right nuisance.

Horrible howlers

Schools have always taught pupils about Rotten Rulers.

But did the pupils really learn much?

They sometimes get things a little bit mixed up. You know the sort of thing – Joan of Arc was Noah's sister.

Or when the teacher asks a question he gets the wrong answer.

WHERE WERE THE KINGS OF ENGLAND CROWNED?

ON THEIR HEADS!

Here are some examples of real mistakes that have been made in English schools.

Queen Elizabeth I was a high born lady. She was born on a mountain.

After the battle of Worcester Charles II fled, disguised as a pheasant.

Lord Nelson was a weak and sickly man. He grew up to be a weak and sickly boy. He died in the battle of Trafalgar Square.

Lady Jane Grey sat on the thorn for nine days

WILLIAM THE CONQUEROR LANDED IN 1066 AD AND AD MEANS 'AFTER DARK'.

In 55 BC Julius Caesar came to Britain but only stayed a short time. The Britons were left to themselves for the next 100 years. Then in AD 43 Caesar came again and conquered Britain.

The Black Prince was killed and taken prisoner.

EDWARD III WOULD HAVE BEEN KING OF FRANCE IF HIS MOTHER HAD BEEN A MAN.

When the Black Prince died it was called the Black Death.

Lady Jane Grey was the grandfather of Henry the ninth.

POTTY PRESIDENTS

Of course not all rulers were just born into power. Some had to be chosen by the people – elected. In the USA, for example, the presidents have to get people to vote for them.

But that doesn't mean they are any better than other Rotten Rulers!

President Franklin Pierce (1853–1857)

Franklin Pierce's problem was booze.

He used one of the worst poster slogans *ever* to get elected. His party, the Democrats, had won with a man named Polk in the last election. So what poster did they come up with this time?

You'll love this.

Poked ... pierced ... Geddit?

Anyway, where was I? Oh, yes. Pickled Pierce.

He spent most of his years in the White House drunk. He even had his own slogan with the US people.

He fell off his horse in the Mexican war, crushed his leg and fainted. His nickname became 'Fainting Frank'.

You've seen the adverts:

Pierce was too drunk to care. He ran over an old woman in 1853 when he was driving drunk. Of course cars hadn't been invented then. He was drunk-driving a horse.

He went to court. He was set free. They said they had to let him go – there were no witnesses. But the truth is they didn't want to arrest a president.

In 1869 his drinking killed him.

Did you know…?

Pierce was the first president to have a Christmas tree in the White House. Sadly there were no kids to enjoy it. His first two children died when they were babies. The third lived – until he was flattened by a railway train just before his dad became president.

Both parents saw it happen. Mother Jane Pierce never got over it – neither did the boy hit by the train, of course.

Pierce's nephews did survive. And his great-great-great-great-nephew became the forty-third US president, George W. Bush.

Ten curious facts about US presidents

Amaze your parents, astound your teachers and send your friends to sleep with these astounding facts, which are no use to anyone.

1 President Ulysses S. Grant (1869–1877) was arrested and fined $20 for speeding in his horse and carriage. The carriage was confiscated and he had to walk back to the White House.

2 William Henry Harrison (1841) served the shortest term ever as US president – 32 days. He made a l-o-n-g speech in a snowstorm, caught pneumonia and died.

3 Franklin Delano Roosevelt's (1933–1945) mother forced him to wear dresses until he was five years old.

4 Bill Clinton (1993–2001) was the first United States president to send an e-mail message. He sent it in March 1993.

5 John Quincy Adams (1825–1829) used to get up before dawn to go swimming naked in the Potomac river.

6 Andrew Johnson Jackson (1829–1837) was the only US president who never went to school and the only president to sew his own clothes. He believed the world was flat – which it is. He was also the only president to kill a man in a duel.

7 At President Andrew Jackson's funeral in 1845, his pet parrot was taken out for swearing. (It didn't go to school either.)

8 Benjamin Harrison (1889–1893) was so afraid of electric lights that he used to get White House staff to turn them on and off for him.

9 William Howard Taft (1909–1913) was the fattest president. He weighed almost 160 kilos. He got stuck in his bath and had to be hauled out. He didn't go on a diet – he just ordered a bigger bath.

10 President Abraham Lincoln (1861–1865) was watching a play when he was assassinated. The play was *Our American Cousin*. It was written by a man from Sunderland, County Durham – just like this book that you are reading. (So watch out for assassins as you read it.)

Phew. That was a close shave. When you turned around to look he ran off and hid. Just as well we warned you.

President Papa Doc Duvalier of Haiti (1907–1971)
At least the US get rid of their potty presidents every few years. In Haiti it was a different story.

Papa Doc wanted all the people in Haiti to vote for him. When they went to vote they had a choice:

The votes were counted. Guess who won?

A few years later he decided he wanted to stay in power for the rest of his life. Again this kind ruler gave his people the choice.

Can you spot what was missing from the voting paper?

Duvalier stayed for life.

President Idi Amin of Uganda (1925–2003)
Amin plotted to take over the whole of Africa. (This potty man kept the heads of his enemies in his fridge. Cool.) He decided to invade the country next door – Tanzania.

President Amin didn't want the Tanzanian army to be ready for him so he sent a friendly message to the Tanzanian President. Very friendly. Very, *very* friendly. It read:

It didn't work and the Tanzanian army easily overcame Amin's attack. And, worse, Amin never got to marry the Tanzanian President.

LOATHSOME LEADER: LUDWIG II OF BAVARIA (1845-1886)

Poor Ludwig was another ruler called 'Mad'.

Why? What did he do that was so mad?

He built castles. He built fantastic castles with steepling towers and halls of mirrors.

They were the sort of castles you see in books of fairy tales. He built castles until Bavaria ran out of money.

Would you believe all the things he did? Have a go.

Get ten out of ten and you, too, could be a mad monarch.

1) Ludwig II was born on the same day as his grandfather King Ludwig I – 25 August. This is exactly what his grandfather wanted. How did this happen?
a) Luck
b) The palace lied about the baby's birthday.
c) His mother was forced to have the baby on that day.

2) Ludwig grew up a bit spoilt. He thought he owned Bavaria. What did the little brat do?
a) Stole a purse
b) Shot a tortoise
c) Sliced off his brother's head

3) Ludwig got a Christmas present that changed his life. What was it?
a) A toy guillotine that let him chop off the heads of mice.
b) A toy cannon that let him blow the legs off the royal throne.
c) A set of building blocks.

4) Ludwig got his love of fairy tales from his mother, who acted them out with local children. But this stopped when a local child behaved badly. What did the child do?
a) Piddled on the palace cat
b) Smacked Ludwig on the lug
c) Stole the crown jewels

5) Ludwig's father treated the boy harshly. How did he make sure Ludwig grew up tough?
a) He starved him.
b) He made him sleep on a raft in the castle moat.
c) He made him run ten miles every day with his hands tied behind his back.

6) When Ludwig took the throne he started building his fairy-tale castles. Linderhof Castle had a concrete cave built beneath it. What was in the cave?
a) Prisoners sent there to be tortured
b) Wild animals in a zoo
c) Rainbows

7) Ludwig's greatest castle was Neuschwanstein. It took 16 years to build. How did Ludwig keep an eye on the building?
a) He walked around it every day.
b) He watched the work through a telescope from a hill across the valley.
c) He set up a tent so he could sleep there.

8) Ludwig began to run out of money. He made plans to get pots of money. What did he intend to do?

a) Rob a bank

b) Invade France and steal French gold

c) Sell his sister as a bride to the Russian king

9) Ludwig did have a slightly potty habit of going on a long ride and having a picnic. What was odd about it?

a) He took no food – just collected squashed hedgehogs from the road and cooked them.

b) He went nowhere – just rode round his stables in endless circles.

c) He hated riding because he was always travel sick; he ate the picnics and threw up.

10) When Ludwig started to act oddly the palace sent for a doctor. What was his name?

a) Baddun

b) Maddun

c) Guddun

Answers:

1b) The baby was born on 24 August 1845, half an hour before midnight. The palace kept quiet about this for an hour and said, 'Guess what? The baby was born half an hour *after* midnight, on his grandad's birthday. Isn't that amazing?'

Grandad King Ludwig I was thrown off his throne three years later. He'd been flirting with the wicked (but beautiful) Lola Montez.[6]

Horrible Histories warning: Keep away from wicked women if you want to keep your crown.

He wrote Lola some dreadful poems. You know the sort of thing…

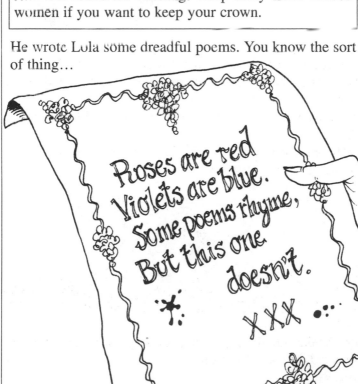

Roses are red
Violets are blue.
Some poems rhyme,
But this one
doesn't.
xxx

6 Some people say Ludwig lost his throne because of a revolt. That is probably true, but it's not so much fun, so it's the Lola Montez story that people remember.

2a) He stole a purse from a shop. His teacher told him he couldn't do that. Ludwig replied:

Everything in Bavaria belongs to me.

He did *not* shoot a tortoise, but he did love his pet tortoise to bits. He loved it so much his father took it from the young prince to teach him a lesson.

Ludwig *was* jealous of little brother Otto. One day Otto made a big snowball and Ludwig snatched it from him. His teacher made him give it back. Ludwig cried:

Why shouldn't I have the snowball? I'm going to be king when I grow up.

And he did *not* cut off his little brother's head, but he was going to! The boys had a row and Ludwig said he could execute his brother. He tied him to a chair and took out a knife. A servant arrived just in time to stop him.

3c) Building blocks were Ludwig's favourite toy. He sat for hours making dream castles. His grandfather watched the boy and said:

The boy is a brilliant artist – a bit like me really.

But once the boy became king he started building the castles for real – even though Bavaria didn't need any more castles.

Shame he wasn't given a train set. Then he could have built something useful for Bavaria like railways.

4b) Ludwig's mother acted out the tales of Hans Christian Andersen. Ludwig himself enjoyed acting – his favourite game was to pretend he was a nun.

Local children joined in the fairy-tale plays and were told to treat Prince Ludwig like one of their friends. One boy, Tony Arco, did just that when he smacked Ludwig's ear.

5a) King Maximilian II gave orders that his sons should never eat till they were full. He didn't want porky princes in his palace. So the boys were fed very little.

They used to go out for a walk in the fields where the farm workers took packed lunches to eat. The boys would beg for food from the workers.

Tough Maximilian II also gave young Ludwig hard beatings if he ever did anything wrong. If a teacher gave a bad report to the King then Ludwig was caned very hard.

The boys were made to get up early every morning and they got very little pocket money.

Ludwig learned to be sneaky. He went off to a dentist to have two teeth removed. He explained:

6c) The cave under Linderhof Castle was built like a fairy world. It had a lake with a hidden machine to make cute little waves. A golden boat bobbed up and down in a rainbow of light.

Ahhhh! Pretty – pretty expensive!

There was also a magic table in the kitchens. The empty table slid below the floor and came up again covered in food.

A hall of mirrors at Herren Chiemsee Palace was 100 metres long. It was lit by 2,200 candles. Ludwig spent just one week living there. Expensive hobby.

7b) Ludwig moved in and spent just 11 days living there. He kept a watch on the builders using a telescope – and that drove them crazy. A bit like your teacher looking over your shoulder when you are trying to do some exciting maths problems. He died before it was finished.

In the end it took 23 years to complete. The castle was copied to build Cinderella's Palace in Disney World.

Ludwig built it to be alone. Now it's packed with thousands of tourists every year.

SO, LITTLE MAN, IS IT TRUE CINDERELLA LIVED HERE?

NO, BUT WE GET A LOT OF VISITS FROM THE UGLY SISTERS

TOUR

8a) Most history books say that Ludwig spent all the taxes of Bavaria and made the people poor. But the history books are wrong – the truth is that Ludwig spent his own money. When he began to run out of money he came up with some brilliant ideas to get more.

One was to stage a bank robbery – that's a pretty honest way to make money. After all, banks rob their customers every day.

Another idea was to kidnap a Prussian Prince. Ludwig would hold him to ransom. Don't try this with your history teacher because (a) they aren't worth enough money to build you a sandcastle and (b) someone may pay you to *keep* them. That is not a good way to make money – history teachers eat a lot.

His last daft idea lost him the throne. He decided to sell Bavaria and buy a smaller kingdom somewhere else. **9b)** Ludwig liked the idea of going on long journeys and stopping off for a picnic. But he never went anywhere – except round and round his stables in circles for hours and hours. He would stop to change horses, have his picnic, then ride on.

10c) He was Dr Guddun (well Gudden to be precise) – except he wasn't a good-un, if you see what I mean.

In 1886 a group of ministers wanted Ludwig off the throne. They sent Dr Bernhard von Gudden to say Ludwig was insane, even though the doctor had not met the King. Ludwig was arrested and taken to Castle Berg on Lake Starnberg.

A few days later Ludwig was dead. He and Gudden went out for a walk on a rainy night and never came home. The next morning their bodies were found in the lake.

No one knows what happened.

Did Ludwig try to kill himself and did Gudden die trying to save him?

Or did Ludwig try to escape and did Gudden die trying to stop him?

Ludwig's cousin, the Empress Elizabeth of Austria said:

The King was not mad; he was just a little odd and lived in a world of dreams. They could have treated him more gently, and maybe saved him from his terrible end.

BE CRUEL TO RULE

If you are going to be a ruler then it helps if you are a bully. Make people obey your silliest wishes. If they don't then have them punished.

Show everyone that *you* are the boss.

What happens if you talk in class? Your teacher shouts at you.

Feeble.

What did Countess Elizabeth Bathory do to her serving girls if they chattered too much?

She sewed their lips together.

Get the idea?

Tamerlane of Mongolia (1336–1405)

Tamerlane (or Timur the Lame or Tamburlaine) was a bit rough on the people he captured. In 1383 he had 2,000 prisoners buried alive at Sabzawar.

Then he had 5,000 beheaded at Zirih and had their heads piled up to make a pyramid.

THIS IS HEADY WORK

You may think this is a sort of sick joke – but Tamerlane didn't like jokes. The penalty for cracking a joke was instant death.

Tsar Paul I of Russia (1754–1801)

If you met the Tsar while he was out driving in his carriage then:

• you had to stop
• you had to get down from your horse or carriage …
• …and lie face down on the ground.

Everyone had to obey this rule. Even if it was snowing they had to throw themselves on to the ground. If you didn't then the Tsar's guards would give you a good beating.

The Tsar had a man called August von Kotzebue arrested and sent to a prison at the Arctic Circle.

The Kotzebue crime? He was a writer – and the Tsar thought all writers were troublemakers. (He could be write there.) Later Kotzebue went to Germany as a Russian spy. He was murdered by a student in 1819. Sometimes it's no fun being a writer. Locked up, frozen and finished.

Tsar Paul ended up strangled on the orders of his own son, Alexander, in 1801. The trouble with being a bully is that sooner or later you meet a bigger bully!

Sultan Mehmed IV of Turkey (1642–1687)
Talking of writers, Mehmed of Turkey had a servant to write a diary of every day of his reign. One day nothing much happened, so Mehmed picked up a spear and stabbed the poor writer with it. He said:

101

Of course Mehmed had a tough life himself. One day, when he was a child, Mehmed cracked a joke that his father, Ibrahim, didn't like.

Ibrahim grabbed his dagger and thrust it in his little son's face.

Mehmed had the scar on his forehead for the rest of his life.

Bad dad.

King Frederick William I of Prussia (1688–1740)

Frederick William liked tall men. His dream was to command an army of giants.

He would do anything to add a tall man to his giant regiment.

He sent officers all around Europe to find them – and he paid parents who handed over their tallest sons.

If a giant refused to join him, Fred Will would have him kidnapped.

But the good news for the giants was that they never had to fight in a battle! Fred Will loved them too much to risk them getting hurt.

They were given an odd little job – when King Fred Will was ill he ordered 100 of his giants to march up and down his bedroom to cheer him up.

King Christian VII of Denmark (1749–1808)

Christian was 17 years old when he took the throne. He was not very grown up. His silly little cruel games included:

- throwing a bowl of sugar over his grandma's head
- sticking pins through her chair to see her jump
- playing leapfrog over the backs of important visitors when they came and bowed in front of him (it wasn't so much fun when he slapped their faces for no reason).

As he grew older he grew more cruel. He had his own Prime Minister executed viciously.

- The man's hand was cut off.
- He was fastened to a wheel and all his bones broken.[7]
- He was beheaded and cut into four pieces.

7 The bones in the chopped-off hand weren't broken, so at least the Prime Minister didn't suffer that. Wasn't he lucky?

103

Savage for servants

Peasants like you have suffered a lot in history. But the people closest to the Rotten Rulers endured the most – the suffering servants.

Sultan Osman II of Turkey (1604–1622)

Thirteen-year-old Osman was very fond of archery – especially when the targets were alive, like prisoners of war or his own page-boys. Osman got his comeuppance later when his troops strangled him and squashed his naughty bits. They cut off his ear and sent it to his mother. Soz Oz.

The Raja of Akhalot – Indian Prince (1800s)

The British Army conquered India and gave the Raja the power to rule Akhalot.

But they couldn't give him brain-power. They began to suspect something was wrong with him when he whipped out a knife one day and lopped off a servant's nose and ears for no apparent reason.

Veddius Pollio (died AD 15)

Not exactly a ruler, but a rich Roman friend of Emperor Augustus. Vicious Ved fed one of his servants to his man-eating eels.

The servant's crime?

He dropped a glass.

104

Ten things you never knew about rulers

1) Peter the Great of Russia had a thing about dwarfs. When two of his favourite dwarfs got married, Peter invited 72 more dwarfs from all over Russia to the wedding. He had little tables and chairs made for them. When one of his dwarfs died, Peter gave him a rich funeral with the small coffin pulled by tiny horses. The funeral was led by a dwarf priest.

2) Attila the Hun was less than 140 cm tall.

3) Chinese Emperor Shih Huang Ti ruled in the 200s BC. He built 270 palaces all linked by tunnels. He was so afraid of being murdered that he slept in a different palace every night. He had a habit of having hands, feet and tongues chopped from people in his palace. He also had 160 teachers beheaded.

4) King Amanullah ruled Afghanistan from 1919 until 1929. He once stayed at London's posh Ritz hotel and saw all the men in the street wore bowler hats. He went home to Afghanistan and tried to pass a law to make all the men in Afghanistan wear bowler hats.

5) In the 1700s King Henry Cristophe ruled northern Haiti. He had a huge snooker table in his palace. He used to hit the white ball into human heads on the table. This is *not* where the ancient joke came from…

Henry Cristophe also ordered his guards to show him how loyal they were. He told them to march over a 60-metre-high cliff. Those who did died. Those who refused were executed.

6) Tsar Paul of Russia loved his dad, Peter III, so much he had him dug up. The corpse was dressed in royal robes, put on a throne and crowned. Peter had been dead 34 years so he must have been a mouldy monarch.

7) Napoleon, Emperor of France, is known as the best general *ever*. But even he got it wrong sometimes. Before the Battle of Waterloo in 1815 he said:

I tell you, the English leader Wellington is a bad general. The English are bad soldiers. We will win this by lunchtime.

He lost.

8) The Sioux Indian Chief, Rain-in-the-face, was present when the Sioux massacred General Custer and the US Cavalry in 1876 (see page 61). While eating Custer's heart he said:

I don't much like the taste. I am only eating this for revenge.

9) The real Count Dracula ruled in Romania from 1456 till 1476. He was horribly cruel. One of his nastiest tricks was to take a group of prisoners of war and have three of them fried alive. The others were then forced to eat them.

10) Foulest fact of all:

Horrible Histories health warning: Reading the next bit can seriously damage your dinner. Do *not* read it. You have been warned!

Henry VIII of England had a servant who had just one job. The servant's job was to follow Henry to the toilet and wipe his fat backside.

HOLY HORRORS

The top ruler of all has to be God, of course.

Being a ruler he can be as rotten as the rest. The God of the Bible sent a flood to drown everything in the world (except Noah's family and a couple of every animal). You don't get much more rotten than that.

God also had his favourite pet peoples. He sent plagues of frogs and locusts and germs to attack their enemies. He is still sending us plagues of things like traffic wardens and American tourists.[8]

WE'VE UPSET SOMEONE!

It is no surprise that a lot of rulers start to think they *are* gods. Of course, that must upset God a bit, so he lets them get away with it for a while before he crushes them like a hedgehog under a 10-ton truck. But for a while these holy horrors can bring misery to millions.

Maharajah Jai Singh of Alwar in India (1892–1937)

This mad maharajah believed he was the god Rama. He spent a lot of time working out how big Rama's crown should be so he could have a copy made.

Rama was a kind and loving god, the maharajah was not.

8 The Greek Gods were kinder and did gentle things like eat their own babies. The Norse gods were just as tender and might tie an enemy to a tree using his own guts for rope. Harmless really.

He:
- lost a polo match, so he took his polo pony, soaked it in petrol and set fire to it
- loved hunting tigers; to get the tigers into the open he used babies for bait – he told the mothers:

I'M A GREAT SHOT. I'LL KILL THE TIGER BEFORE IT EATS YOUR BABY. AND EVEN IF I MISS, THE CHILD WON'T FEEL A THING. TIGERS KILL VERY QUICKLY

OH, THAT'S ALL RIGHT THEN!

He also:
- liked to tie boys to the back of an ox cart and watch as they were dragged through the village
- enjoyed shooting at pet dogs
- thought he was greater than the King of Britain – well, a god is greater than the King of Britain. The maharajah refused to take his gloves off when he shook hands with the King – a huge insult.

WHAT A CHEEK!

In the end the British Army threw the maharajah out of India. His punishment? He had to live in Paris with only 20 servants to care for him. Poor, sad god – not as poor or sad as the flaming pony, of course.

Benito Mussolini of Italy (1883–1945)

Benito was a mate of Adolf Hitler and nearly as nasty.

The greatest hero in Roman legend was Hercules – a super-strong god. Mussolini decided to have a statue of himself built. He ordered a statue of himself dressed as Hercules.

The statue was to be 80 metres tall – even mighty Hercules wasn't that big!

President Papa Doc Duvalier of Haiti (1907–1971)

General Blucher Philogenes led a revolt against President Papa Doc Duvalier in 1963. The revolt failed and Philogenes was beheaded.

But that was not the end of his story. Papa Doc didn't think he was a god, but he used god-like 'magical powers' to help him to run the country. He was into voodoo magic.

Duvalier ruled with the help of a gang of murdering thugs. They were called the 'Tonton Macoute'.

'The who?' I hear you ask.

Well, little Haitian children believed in a sort of Santa Claus. They called him 'Uncle Tonton' and thought he brought them presents at Christmas.

But if children were naughty they thought they would be snatched by the evil uncle and stuffed in his sack – Tonton Macoute was the evil 'Uncle Sack'.

That was the name given to the murder gangs. Their job was to look after Papa Doc at all costs.

For some reason they all had to wear sunglasses.

The Tonton Macoute banned the boy scouts because some scouts once wrote 'Down with Doc' on a wall. Anyone in the scouts was punished by death.

They hanged their victims in public to terrify the people.

President Kim Il Sung of North Korean (1912–1994)

Who is the President of North Korea? Kim Il Sung – even though he died in 1994.

Who will be president of Korea 100 years from now? Kim Il Sung. He is president *for ever*.

How can a dead man still be president? Easy. He is a god. At least, that's what the Koreans believe.

Kim led them to freedom from Japanese rule in the 1940s and he became a sort of superhero. Here's how to make yourself a god:

9 Of course the song meant the 'bombs' were people willing to die for him. They wouldn't actually explode in a battle because that would be too messy.

113

During Kim's rule, three million people died from war and famine – but that's not his fault, is it?

Emperor Domitian of Rome (ruled AD 81–96)
Domitian was a quite decent man at first – well, compared to other Roman Emperors, that is.

Sadly, in his later years he became a proper prawn.

He began to think of himself as a god and made a new rule…

He then had gold statues of himself sent to all parts of the Empire.

Did you know…?

1) Villagers in the New Hebrides Islands (in the Pacific Ocean) worship the Duke of Edinburgh (husband of Queen Elizabeth II).

They think that one day he will cure them of every sickness and they will live for ever.

Won't they be disappointed when they are nailed down in their coffins?

2) King and Queens often have holy water sprinkled on their heads when they are crowned. This is a blessing from God. King Henry Cristophe of Northern Haiti in the 1700s was blessed with chocolate syrup.

Gooey.

A potted history of popes

Sometimes religious leaders are also Rotten Rulers. Popes are the leaders of the Catholic Church and for hundreds of years they ruled over the powerful papal states. They are God's representatives on Earth and are supposed to be good men. They weren't always, though.

- Pope Damasus (AD 366–384) got the job by sending his thugs to beat his rival to death. They also murdered the man's friends. It worked.
- Pope John XII (AD 955–963) didn't believe in God. He enjoyed worshipping the Devil. He was beaten to death by a hammer – probably by a friend of God.

- Pope Stephen VII (AD 896–897) had the corpse of Pope Formosus dug up and put on trial. A pope raises three fingers to bless people – these fingers were cut off the corpse before it was thrown into the river.
- Pope John XIII (AD 965–972) liked a Roman statue of Emperor Marcus Aurelius on a horse. The Pope used the statue to hang one of his enemies by the hair. John XIII was later battered to death.
- Pope Gregory VII (1073–85) was a midget who tried to *ban* Christians from reading the Bible. He said that reading the Bible might start them thinking. And, as you know, thinking is a bad thing. Don't do it.

- Pope Boniface VIII (1294–1305) locked up Pope Celestine V and left him to starve to death. It was said Boniface later killed himself and his body was dug up by Pope Clement V and burned.
- Pope Alexander VI (1492–1503) started his criminal career very young. He murdered someone when he was just 12 years old. Alexander's son tried to poison a couple of priests at a dinner. Alexander drank the poison by mistake and died. Oooops!
- Pope Paul III (1534–1549) had an argument with a Polish bishop about religion. The Pope won the argument by poisoning the bishop.

POLISH BISHOP   POLISH OFF

Did you know…?
Pope Adrian IV (1100–1159) was the only Englishman ever to rule the Catholic Church. He was also the only one to die in this horrible way. What way did God decide to polish off his prime priest?

a) Adrian choked when he swallowed a fly.

b) Adrian's head was crushed when a dead albatross fell from the sky.

c) Adrian was bitten on the bot by a Sydney Funnel-Web Spider that was hiding under his toilet seat.

The Grand Lama of Tibet (since 1578)

This man was so holy that every bit of him had the power of a god – even his poo and his pee.

His followers wore lumps of his dried poo around their necks. They mixed his pee with their food. They thought it would make women love them.

Li Chih-ch'ang (died 1227)

Li Chih-ch'ang was a Buddhist leader. There are *two* stories told about his death. His friends said:

But his enemies told a different tale – and probably the truth!

TERRIBLY TRUE OR FANTASTICALLY FALSE?

Sometimes it's hard to believe the way Rotten Rulers behaved. But can you tell the real life from the lies? Just answer 'True' or 'False' to these odd facts.

1) When Jean-Bédel Bokassa (1921–1996) of the Central African Republic was not murdering and eating children he was collecting stamps as a hobby.
2) Pope John XXI (ruled 1276–1277) got the job because he was a doctor, not a priest.
3) Alexander the Great (356–323 BC) made the world's first rope bridge.
4) Frederick the Great of Prussia (1712–1786) is remembered for his sweet scent.
5) Ivan the Terrible (1530–1584) ordered the Archbishop of Novograd to be sewn into a bear skin.

6) An old woman saved her own life by promising a Mongol a pearl that she had swallowed.
7) Tamerlane the Great (1336–1405) defeated an enemy at sea without a fight.
8) Delhi was ruled by a sultana in 1236.
9) Murad IV of Turkey (1612–1640) forced his enemies to smoke themselves to death.
10) In 1591 Prince Dmitri of Russia (1350–1389) cut his own throat by accident.

Answers:

1) True. He even gave himself a title to make him the world's greatest stamp collector: 'Grand Master of the International Brotherhood of Knights Collectors of Postage Stamps.'

2) True. Three popes had died in five years. The Church decided it needed a fit man who could look after himself and would last a little longer. John was a doctor. He was fit. Sadly his fitness did not help when the roof of his palace fell down on his head.

3) False. When ruthless Al needed a bridge he wrecked a village, threw it in the river and his army walked across it. The villagers were left homeless, of course.

4) False. Frederick is remembered for (a) starting endless wars and (b) smelling horrible.

5) True. Hunting dogs, trained to kill bears, were sent to tear him apart.

BEAR SKIN, YOU FOOLS. I SAID **BEAR** SKIN!

6) False. The soldier killed her and cut her open to get the pearl – quicker than waiting for her to poo the pearl. His leader, Genghis Khan then ordered all the corpses to be cut open in search of treasure.

7) True. Tamerlane had defeated the city of Smyrna. A fleet of Smyrna's allies set sail to attack him. Tamerlane lopped off the heads of the soldiers. He had them floated out to sea on candlelit dishes. The invader got the message.

8) True. Razia of Delhi in India was chosen by the sultan to rule from 1236 to 1240 because her brothers were a waste of space. But a 'sultan' is a man – she was Delhi's first lady-sultan or 'sultana'.

GEE, HONEY, WAS THERE REALLY A SULTANA ON THIS THRONE?

NO, HONEY, IT'S A CURRANT

A CURRENT? I DIDN'T KNOW THEY HAD ELECTRIC CHAIRS IN THOSE DAYS

9) False. Murad IV *hated* smoking. He hated it so much he banned it from Turkey and had any smoker executed on the spot. His soldiers were beheaded or cut into quarters. If they smoked on the battlefield then they had their hands and feet crushed and were left for the enemy to finish off. Which just goes to show…

10) False. Dmitri's wicked guardian *said* that Dmitri had been playing with a knife, had a fit and fell on the knife. If you are daft enough to believe that then the answer is 'true'. But the Russians knew he'd been murdered. They attacked and killed the men who were supposed to guard Prince Dmitri. The little prince was only nine years old.

LOATHSOME LEADER: MURAD IV OF TURKEY (1612~1640)

Murad IV of Turkey was five years old, when his father died. Six years later he took the throne from his potty uncle, Mad Mustafa.

By the time he died his people must have been glad to see the back of him – and the corpse of him.

If one of his bodyguards had written home, his letter might have told the terrible tale like this:

Dear Mum,

Well, the good news is I am still alive. I don't know how. The better news is that Murad is dead. Yes, I know, amazing isn't it? I was just saying to my friend, Bayezid, I said 'Bayezid,' that's his name, I said, 'Bayezid, it's hard to believe.' And Bayezid said he didn't believe it either! 'I don't believe it either,' he said. We've been with Murad ever since he took the throne back in, ooooh, let me see, 1623. He was only 11. Cute as a kitten! And you know what kittens do to little birds.

He hated his Prime Minister (what we call the Grand Vezir) and had him executed. Well, we didn't like him much either, so that was no problem. Quick swish of the scimitar and off with his ugly head.

But then Murad wanted the Vezir's friends killed. All 500 of them.

We had to strangle them. You know what it's like strangling a chicken, Mum? Well, strangling those men was much harder. My arms ached for days.

Then we set off round Baghdad, looking for spies and Murad said, "If you find one, kill him - or her."

No trial, mind you. Find and kill. Just like that.

I have to say it was fun at first. But over in Anatolia he wanted 20,000 executed and that was *not* fun. I said to Bayezid, ' It took me days to get the blood out of my uniform.'

Still, if Murad ordered it, we had to do it. Oh, but he was a big, dark-eyed brute. Loved wrestling and throwing spears around the palace.

125

One day Murad's brother threw Murad down in a wrestling match. Mad? Murad went redder than a lump of Turkish Delight. He called us to him and told us to kill his brother. His OWN brother. Another two brothers were pushed off the perch four years ago. There's only one brother left - Mad Ibrahim - and that's who we're stuck with now. Murad certainly kept us busy with all his wars.

In Baghdad in 1638 we massacred 30,000 soldiers and then 30,000 women and children inside the city. Hard work, but as Bayezid said, 'Better than them killing us'.

I can't say this now he's dead - Murad turned a bit peculiar towards the end. He made me his chief executioner, and him and me used to disguise ourselves.

Then we wandered the streets looking for criminals. When he found one I had to execute him. The people were a bit upset by all those crooks strung up at street corners.

Bayezid says there was less crime in those days. 'But Bayezid,' I said. 'He went a bit far. We were executing people for daft reasons in the end.'

My friend Bayezid said, 'Yes I remember you had to execute Murad's musician for playing a song from Persia - the enemy.' And then Murad banned smoking, booze and coffee. I was at it day and night, chopping chaps who were caught with a pipe. The thing is, Mum, Murad smoked like a volcano and drank like a camel. (Except a camel drinks water, but you know what I mean.)

As I say I am glad to be alive but even gladder that you are still alive.

Murad got to hate women. He used to practise his archery on women in the streets. He once came across a group of women singing in a meadow and having a picnic.

'I hate that noise', he said. 'Drown them in the river.'

Oh, but they struggled, I can tell you.

127

I was worn out and wet through.
Even his wives were forced to jump in
a palace pool. Then he fired pellets
at them. You should have heard them
scream - the ones that weren't drowning
that is.
At night he wandered the streets in
his nightshirt and killed anyone he saw.
   He really liked chopping the heads off
men with fat necks. Don't ask me why.
   But he's dead now. The doctors say it
was the booze that killed him - the
booze he killed other people
for drinking!
   So it serves him right
in a way.
   He was only 27.
   I'm off down the tavern with
my friend Bayezid for a few cups of wine.
   I just hope this mad Ibrahim isn't
as bad as his big brother.
Take care and enjoy your picnic.
Just don't do any singing or I may have
to drown you.
(Only joking Mum. Ha! Ha!)

your Loving Son Ahmed xxx

TRY TO LIE

If you want to be a ruler then it's very handy to be able to *cheat* and *lie*.

Nasty Nazi leader Adolf Hitler said:

Most people fall for BIG lies, not small ones.

Herr Hitler's big lie was that the Jews were to blame for most German problems: get rid of the Jews and Germany would be a happier place.

Rubbish, of course, but sadly most people at that time believed his big lie and millions died.

Here are a few foul fibbers.

Malik Andeel
This Ethiopian slave wanted to be ruler of Bengal in northern India. But Bareek was his lord and Malik had sworn an oath.

I PROMISE TO DEFEND MY LORD BAREEK ON HIS THRONE

So he couldn't kill Bareek, could he?

Actually, he could. One night he got Bareek very drunk and the fat lord fell asleep in a chair. Malik Andeel and his friends stabbed their lord to death and Malik took his place.

I SWORE TO DEFEND MY LORD BAREEK ON HIS THRONE. BUT HE'S NOT ON HIS THRONE, IS HE?

OOOOH! THAT'S CRAFTY, THAT IS!

Sultan Abdul Hamid II of Turkey (1842–1918)
Abdul Hamid didn't want his people to think rulers could be assassinated – they might try it on him! So, when he had the King and Queen of Serbia murdered he made the Turkish newspapers print a whopping lie:

The Turkey Times

King and Queen of Serbia die from indigestion

Indigestion? They were attacked in their palace by 50 army officers. They were chopped into pieces and the pieces were thrown out of the windows.

That's enough to give anyone a bad tummy.

Chairman Mao Tse-Tung of China (1893–1976)
Mao started life as a teacher (so he got a lot of practice at being a dictator).

He had millions of his enemies killed.

But that would make him look wicked, wouldn't it? So his executioners were ordered to make the deaths look like accidents or suicides.

A popular method was for the victim to 'fall' off the top of a tall building.

Other victims died in front of trains, drowned in lakes or were hanged.

There were so many bodies piling up, they had to wait three days to be cremated. How boring is that, eh? Having to wait for your own burial.

Tsar Peter the Great of Russia (1672–1725)

Peter had trouble with rebel lords. He was sure the rebels were led by his own son, Alexis.

131

So Peter wrote a loving letter to his son.

Dear Alexis
    Come home my dear son. I know you had nothing to do with the rebels. And even if you did I forgive you.
There is nothing to fear.
Come back to your dear old father and let's be friends.
    yours faithfully Dad

Alexis returned.

TORTURE HIM TO GET THE TRUTH

THANKS, DAD

NOW EXECUTE HIM!

SORRY, BOSS, THE TORTURE KILLED HIM

YOU CLUMSY OAF!

THAT'S RIGHT, DAD. YOU TELL HIM!

Cheat to beat

If you want to be a leader, you might have to do a bit of cheating as well as lying. If you want to be a really top terror, then you probably need to do a *lot* of cheating and lying and clever tricks. Here's a quick terrible test from Asia in the 1200s.

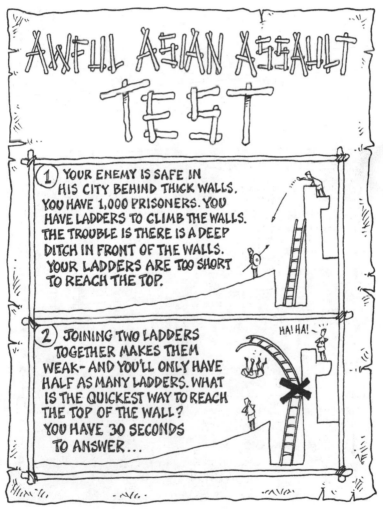

> *Answer:* Drive the prisoners into the ditch. Massacre them with swords and arrows. When the ditch is full of corpses then put your ladders on the corpses and attack. Simple.

What other sly skills can you learn from those in power in the past?

Shah Nadir of Persia (1688–1747)

It's the oldest trick in the book. You just *have* to use it if you are going to be a leader. You probably use it already.

First you pretend to be nice to your enemies, get them to trust you.

Then you hit them.

Here is an example:

It is called the 'sucker punch' (though you don't really have to punch them to give it).

Nadir was the son of a poor peasant, but he went on to rule Persia. How did he do it?

In 1725 Nadir wanted power in the state of Isfahan. So he didn't struggle against the great men, he buttered them up and then hit them with the sucker punch. First he said:

134

This sort of scene has happened time and time again in history, but people still fall for it. Don't be afraid to try this popular old trick. It *still* works.

Deborah of Israel

Debbie was a judge, a prophet and a war leader. (Where did she find the time?)

She had trouble with the Canaanites – well, we all have trouble spelling their name.

Anyway, they had great war chariots and they were going to cut Debbie's Israeli army to bits because her men were on foot.

So what did daring Debs do? She led her army up a rocky hill. The Canaanite chariots clattered and crunched their way up the hill, but lost their wheels and smashed the spokes.

The Israeli army charged down and chopped them. Easy. Now why didn't you think of that?

Li Yuan Ho of Tibet

Li Yuan Ho was a Tibetan chief. In 1038 his greatest enemy were the Song. And he knew the Song would be entering a valley where his men could massacre them.

How would LYH's men know when the Song were in the valley? Here's how:

QUAINT QUIZ

Think you know anything about leaders? Then test your brain-power with this quick quiz.

If you are clever you'll get ten out of ten. If you are a great leader you will get 11 out of ten.

1) Louis XIV of France (1638–1715) had a girlfriend, Madame de Montespan. When he got bored with her she fed him a magic love drink. What was in it?
a) Toad poo
b) Toad warts
c) Toad blood

2) Gian Gastone (1671–1737) was ruler of Tuscany. He was a drunkard, and when he drank he threw up. What did he use to wipe his spew-stained mouth?
a) His socks
b) His pet cat
c) His wig

3) General Kitchener of Great Britain (1850–1916) dug up the skull of the Mahdi of Sudan. It was a bit of revenge. Queen Victoria made him bury it again. Kitchener had been using the skull to hold what?
a) Ink
b) Soup
c) His pet caterpillars

4) Ibrahim I 'The Mad' of Turkey (1616–1648) was a jealous man. He heard that one of his wives had another boyfriend. But he didn't know which wife. What did he do?

a) Divorced them all

b) Drowned them all

c) Blinded them all

5) The rulers of Irian Jaya in Indonesia would hang above the roofs of the village houses. Why?

a) They were dead.

b) They were bird-spotting.

c) They were rat-catching.

6) The Russian royal family had a favourite monk called Rasputin. He was a peasant and often shocked people at feasts by doing what?

a) Filling his mouth with wine and spitting it back into the cup (to warm it up)

b) Picking his nose and using snot balls instead of salt

c) Eating fish soup with his bare hands (very grubby hands at that!)

7) Why is a soccer ball the size of a human head?

a) Because King Henry III of England passed a law saying all footballs must be the size of his head

b) Because the first football game in England was played with the lopped-off head of a Viking lord

c) Because Roman footballs were made from the skin of a human head, sewn up and filled with air

139

8) When Russian leader Josef Stalin died in 1953, about 500 other Russians died. How?
a) They were blown up with the bomb that killed him.
b) They were so upset they starved themselves to death.
c) They were trampled to death in the crush to see his body at the funeral.

9) President Idi Amin of Uganda (1925–2003) had many people murdered. But he worried that his minister Michael Ondanga would come back and haunt him. How did Amin try to stop the murdered Ondanga returning as a ghost?
a) He had a ton of garlic scattered round the dead man's grave.
b) He had part of the dead man's liver cut out and ate it.
c) He left a note in the coffin saying he would kill Ondanga's family if he ever rose from the grave.

10) Chairman Mao Tse-Tung (or Mao Zedong) of China (1893–1976) ran the country so badly that the crops failed and millions of people began to starve. It was Mao's fault. What did Mao blame?
a) Alien visitors – they were stealing corn to power their flying saucers
b) Television – workers were watching when they should have been weeding
c) Sparrows – they were eating the corn before it was ripe

Answers:

1a) Toad poo. If you want someone to fall in love with you, and you don't have any toad poo handy, then other rulers had other odd ideas you could try. For example, sheep's eyelids soaked in tea (Chinese emperors) or crushed animal glands (Hitler). Maybe you'd enjoy what kings in the Middle Ages learned to love – a mixture of powdered pigeon poo and snail poo; the snails made sure it didn't work too fast. Pope John XXI used pig poo to shove up the nostrils to stop a nosebleed.

2c) Gian Gastone had some disgusting habits. His dogs shared his bed and it smelled of pipe-smoke, booze, vomit and poo. His sister-in-law tried to keep it clean but she died – wouldn't you? As he grew older he became blind and let his nails and beard grow till he looked disgusting. He probably scared his dogs.

3a) Kitchener used it as an inkwell. The Mahdi had killed Kitchener's friend General Gordon. But the Mahdi died before Kitchener could get his own back, so he blew up the Mahdi's tomb and pinched the skull. Before the days of ball-point pens most schoolchildren used inkwells – but none as gruesome as Kitchener's. Ask your grandma what she used.

4b) Ibrahim decided to have all of his 280 wives thrown into the Bosphorus river. They were tied up in sacks with stones. One girl escaped, because her sack had been badly tied up. She was rescued by the sailors of a French ship. After too many cruel acts like this Ibrahim was locked in a cage; he ended up strangled with a bow string.

5a) When a ruler died he was hung over a smoking fire for a few months. This stopped his corpse from going rotten and turned him into a smoky mummy. He was then hung from the roof of his palace so he could watch over the village and look after his people.

School pupils who smoke round the back of the gym could end up mummified.

6c) Rasputin had terrible manners and was filthy. His long, black beard was stained with food and probably smelled like a dustbin. He was very popular with women (honest!).

HE'S GREAT. I CAN HAVE A SNOG AND A MEAL AT THE SAME TIME

Of course, a lot of Russian rulers were no better. Tsar Peter the Great (1672–1725) had awful manners, too. He often trampled over the dinner table, crushing food under his filthy feet.

7b) Legend has it that the Viking raider was lopped and his head kicked around. The Saxon slayers enjoyed it so much they wanted to keep on playing the game – but the dead head fell apart. They made a new ball from pig guts, but it had to be the same size as the Viking head.

And, amazingly, in 2001 a Swede became head of English football again.

8c) Thousands of people lined up in the snow to see Stalin's corpse on display at the Moscow Hall of Columns. The crowds were so thick that some people were trampled underfoot when they slipped on the snow. Others were crushed against traffic lights, and some choked to death. Around 500 Russians died trying to get one last look at their hero.

9b) Evil Amin killed around 300,000 of his own people, including his wife. The heads of his enemies were fed to crocodiles. When Queen Elizabeth II had been on the British throne for 25 years, Amin said:

I EXPECT ELIZABETH TO SEND ME A PRESENT - I THINK SHE WILL SEND ME SOME OF HER 25-YEAR-OLD KNICKERS

She didn't. He must have been disappointed.

He was also disappointed when the Scots turned down a kind offer from him – he said he would be King of Scotland and lead them to freedom.

The Brit Prime Minister called him 'a madman and a buffoon'.

10c) Mao blamed sparrows for eating the Chinese corn. It wasn't true – the sparrows would have been too fat to fly if they'd eaten enough corn for a billion people. Chinese peasants were ordered to bang gongs for two days so the sparrows flew up in a flap. The sparrows dropped dead from lack of sleep. It worked – sparrows died, but the sparrows had been killing the insects that ate the crops. The insects had a lovely time and the famine grew worse than ever.

Mao grew fat.

LOATHSOME LEADER: GENGHIS KHAN - WARLORD OF MONGOLIA [10] (1167~1227)

Little Temujin had a tough childhood. He grew up to lead the Mongol people to conquer a huge part of the world – he probably ruled a larger area than any other leader in history. And you don't do that by being nice to grannies and giving lollipops to kids.

Temujin changed his name to Genghis because it means 'Perfect Warrior', and became 'Torturer Len'[11] because that means 'Perfectly Nasty Sort of Leader'.

When he died, his empire stretched from the Yellow Sea to the Black Sea (with lots of blue seas of water and red seas of blood in between).

We know all about gruesome Genghis because a l-o-n-g poem was written about him shortly before he died. You wouldn't want to read it (it's in ancient Mongolian anyway). So here's a *Horrible Histories* version.

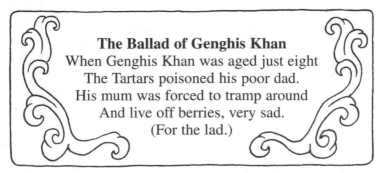

The Ballad of Genghis Khan
When Genghis Khan was aged just eight
The Tartars poisoned his poor dad.
His mum was forced to tramp around
And live off berries, very sad.
(For the lad.)

10 What do you mean, 'Where is Mongolia?' This is not a geography book. Go and look it up in an Atlas you idle reader.
11 Unscramble the letters of 'Torturer Len' to see what I mean. I'm not doing it for you. It took me three days to scramble them in the first place.

At 13 years he caught some birds,
His brother fancied them to eat.
They argued. Genghis killed his bruv.
At least he had some nice fresh meat.
(Or tweet.)

At 20 years he took a bride,
A jealous tribe snatched her away.
Our Genghis formed a little army,
Rescued her and won the day.
(Hooray!)

Jamukha was the Mongol chief
Until he with Genghis tangled.
A big mistake, he lost the fight,
And our Genghis had him strangled.
(Mangled.)

Now Genghis said, 'I was so good
At fighting Mongols in this war,
I'll roam around the great big world
And try to conquer more and more!'
(Oh, lor!)

In twelve-o-nine he started out
Attacking China. Lots of slaughter.
Chinese king said, 'Go away. I'll
Pay you camels and my daughter!'
(Did he oughter?)

In twelve-two-one Khan headed west,
The town of Merv stood in his way.
The people fought, but lost at last.
Khan killed a million in a day.[12]
(Slay! slay!)

By twelve-two-seven Khan was dead;
Some say he fell from off his horse.
Others say a princess stabbed him.
Heck, she must have used some force.
(Of course.)

The Mongol armies moved on west,
(On horseback 'cos they liked to ride.)
Smashed the Russians and went on to
Europe, which was terrified.
('Help!' they cried.)

But with Genghis gone they argue,
Mongols break up, empires fall.
All that murder, all that bloodshed,
What was all that killing for?
(No more).

12 It may have been as many as 1,300,000 unarmed men, women and children that were massacred in Merv. Of course Genghis didn't kill them himself. Each Mongol soldier killed about three or four hundred helpless people that day.

Feast like a leader

Want to eat food fit for a king? (Or fit for a Khan?)

Then try Genghis Khan's recipe. In 1202 he was on the run from his enemies and starving. He and his friends survived with the help of a horse.

Here's the recipe.

SURVIVAL STEW

GOT A PROBLEM STAYING ALIVE IN THE EMPTY GRASSLANDS OF MONGOLIA? HERE'S OUR CHEF'S TOP TIP TO GET YOU THROUGH WITH A SUPER SURVIVAL STEW

① FIRST, CATCH A HORSE AND KILL IT...

② NOW SKIN THE HORSE CAREFULLY SO YOU DON'T SPLIT THE SKIN...

③ GUT THE HORSE AND THROW AWAY THE GUTS...

④ FILL THE SKIN WITH WATER. LIGHT A FIRE AND PLACE LARGE STONES IN THE FIRE...

⑤ PLACE THE HOT STONES IN THE WATER SO IT BOILS...

⑥ PUT THE HORSE FLESH IN THE BOILING WATER TILL IT IS COOKED...

⑦ EAT AND ENJOY YOUR TASTY STEW...

Genghis and his friends had to cook in muddy water, but it gave them the strength to go out and conquer the world.

No horses? The Mongols were starving at the siege of Beijing in 1214. Disease killed thousands of men. It was said that they ate the corpses.

HORRIBLE H'ENDS

Tsar Peter III of Russia discovered that his wife Catherine had a boyfriend. He had the boyfriend's head chopped off and put in a jar. Catherine was then forced to have the jar at her bedside wherever she went.

That is Rotten Ruling.

If you are going to be a Rotten Ruler you need to think of new ways to kill people. People will *remember* you if you do that.

Get the idea?

Go and think of your own ways to kill people. Here are some examples to give you some ideas.

Emperor Alexander Severus of Rome (ruled AD 222–135)

Emperor Elagabalus planned to have his nephew Alexander killed. But Alexander's friends started killing off Elagabalus's assassins first.

They didn't just chop them up or poison them. They made sure they died slowly.

They held them down, slit them open, then pulled out their guts, their livers, their lungs and their hearts.

Sultan Selim II of Turkey (ruled 1566–1574)

Selim loved booze. He really, *really* loved Cyprus wine. But one day he ran out of his favourite tipple.

Horror! 'What can I do to get some more?' he whined.

'Take over Cyprus,' his friends told him.

So he invaded Cyprus. Thirty thousand people died in the battles.

Finally the leader of the Cypriot army, Bragadino, was captured. He was skinned alive. His skin was stuffed with straw and paraded in front of the troops from Turkey.[13]

President Idi Amin of Uganda (1925–2003)

President Idi Amin had his enemies arrested by the police and then shot with machine guns. The trouble was, the machine guns made a lot of noise and the local people couldn't get to sleep. So the police came up with a new way of execution. The prisoners were given a seven-kilo sledgehammer and told:

Prisoners had to take it in turn to kill another prisoner with the hammer – and then be killed themselves.

13 It is usually the Turkey that is stuffed and paraded on the Christmas dinner table. If you paraded a man in front of the Turkeys then imagine how they would cheer.

151

Kim Jong Il of Korea (ruled 1994–today)

You want chemical weapons that you can use to bomb your enemies, but how do you know they will work? Test them on prisoners in your jails.

In the 1990s reports came from North Korea saying that prisoners were being shut in a glass case, then gas was pumped into the case.

The chemist could then watch the prisoners die and see how well a gas worked.

One chemist was a bit shocked. He said:

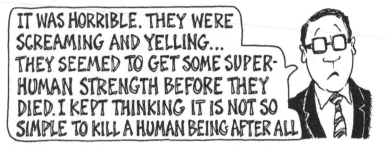

IT WAS HORRIBLE. THEY WERE SCREAMING AND YELLING... THEY SEEMED TO GET SOME SUPER-HUMAN STRENGTH BEFORE THEY DIED. I KEPT THINKING IT IS NOT SO SIMPLE TO KILL A HUMAN BEING AFTER ALL

But the chemists did it because Kim Jong Il told them to.

Genghis Khan of Mongolia (1167–1227)

Mongol warlord Genghis Khan won a battle then discovered that the enemy warlord was an old friend. He said:

I WILL NOT SHED THE BLOOD OF AN OLD FRIEND

THAT IS THE SIGN OF A GREAT AND JUST LEADER

And that's what they did.

Alexander 'The Wolf' of Badenoch in Scotland (1343–1405)

Awful Alex ruled the north of Scotland and had a nasty habit of hunting in the Ruthiemurchus Forest. He set fire to parts of it to drive out the deer so he could kill them. He also enjoyed hunting outlaws in the same way.

When he caught a victim he stood him in a cellar in a metre of icy water.

If the prisoner stood up he would live – if he tried to sit down or fell asleep, he would drown.

It was left there for two or three days. If he lived then he would be set free.

Robert III of Scotland (1337–1406)

Robert had a lot of trouble with Scottish clans, who wouldn't stop fighting. To solve the problem he came up with a clever idea.

In 1396 he organized a contest on the North Inch of Perth. Robert and a huge crowd watched as 30 men of the Clan Davidson fought against 30 men of the MacPherson clan.

The fight was to the death.

Each man was dressed in a short kilt and armed with sword, dagger, axe, crossbow and three arrows.

Bagpipes played and the men slaughtered each other until at the end of the day only a dozen were still alive.

They were all badly wounded.

Of course the dead and wounded had been the worst troublemakers in Scotland. After that it was much more peaceful in the Scottish Highlands.

Emperor Domitian of Rome (AD 51–96)

Daft Domitian grew madder and crueller the longer he ruled. He would ask a victim, 'What death are you most afraid to die?'

Whatever the victim said, Domitian would arrange it.

Of course if you knew this you could cheat him, couldn't you?

Domitian also loved to torture men to death.

One of his favourite nasty tricks was to chain the victim to a wall. Then the Emperor would hold a flaming torch under the man's naughty bits before cutting them off.

He then watched as the poor man bled to death.

Emperor Tiberius of Rome (ruled AD 14–37)
This bad-tempered man was easily upset. And if you upset him he'd have your ears cut off and fed to his lions.

He became so annoyed with one of his wives that he had her locked in the bathroom, then ordered his servants to turn up the heat.

She was steamed to death.

Emperor Wenceslas of Germany (ruled 1378–1400)
Wenceslas was angry with his chef for cooking him a mouldy meal. The Emperor ordered him to be executed. The chef was taken away and roasted alive on his own kitchen spit.

Ten ways you wouldn't want to die

Now that you've read this book you will know how to be a leader. But there's one thing you need to know before you try: *leaders die too!*

And a lot of leaders have come to some very nasty ends.

King Mithridates IV of Asia Minor (ruled 112–63 BC)
The poet A.E. Housman wrote a comic poem about King Mithridates and the plots to kill him.

They put arsenic in his meat
And stared aghast to watch him eat;
They poured strychnine in his cup
And shook to see him drink it up:
They shook, they stared as white
as their shirt:
Them it was their poison hurt.
– I tell the tale that I heard told.
Mithridates, he died old.

But the end of the poem is not quite true. And it doesn't explain *how* the King ate the poisons and lived. Here is the *Horrible Histories* truth

Mithridates was sure they were out to get him. 'They hate me. They will try to poison me,' he told his doctor. 'How can I stop them?'

'Poison yourself,' the doctor told him.

'You what? I don't want to die.'

'So, poison yourself. Take a little bit of poison every day. Your body will get used to it. Then, if someone puts

156

poison in your food, it won't kill you,' the doctor told him.

'Really?'

'Really.'

So Mithridates took poison and lived. Until –

'The Romans are coming!' his spies told him.

'They hate me,' he said. 'They'll torture me horribly. What can I do?'

'Poison yourself,' they told him. 'You'll be dead before they get to you.'

'Good idea,' the crafty King said. So he took poison.

It didn't work.

He took more poison.

It didn't work. Well, it wouldn't would it? His doctor had told him that.

'What am I going to do?' he moaned.

'Use a sword,' his girlfriend said, and held out a nice sharp blade.

'It'll hurt!' the King argued.

'Not much, and not for long,' the woman sighed. 'Give it here.'

And she chopped till Mithridates dropped.

Did you know...?

Emperor Napoleon of France had been captured and was really fed up. So in 1814 he decided to kill himself. He drank poison, but that just gave him pains in the gut. Then he decided to shoot himself, but his servant had emptied the gunpowder out of his pistols. Napoleon gave up and decided to stay alive.

He eventually escaped and started another war.

Thousands died at battles like Waterloo in 1815. It would have been much better if the little troublemaker had managed to top himself after all!

King Edmund II 'Ironside' of England (AD 989–1016)

King Edmund went to a feast. He needed the toilet (as you do).

The little boys' room was the only place he went without his bodyguard. It was the only place his enemy could kill him.

What happened next is a mystery. All we know is that Ed became Ded.

Some say a man called Edric Streona hid in the toilet pit and stabbed the King as he sat down, but…

According to another story there was a loaded bow and arrow in the toilet. When the King sat down the bow went off and sent an arrow up into his guts. But…

However, everyone agrees that Edmund Ironside definitely died in the toilet.

Still, no one could figure out what happened to the murderer. It seems Edric Streona went to Edmund's greatest enemy to claim a reward. That enemy was Cnut the Viking. Cnut told him, 'I will raise you higher than any lord in England.'

Then he either...

- cut off Edric Streona's head and had it stuck on the top turret of his castle *or*
- had Edric Streona hanged from the highest tree in the forest.

Did you know?

The Mongol leader Ambakai Khan was captured by his Chinese Jin enemies. He was crucified on a wooden frame they called a 'wooden donkey'. He died slowly. He died so slowly that he had time to send a message to his friends:

Get revenge for me. Get revenge until your five fingers are smashed to splinters. Till your ten fingers drop off!

Frederick William I of Prussia (1688–1740)

When he was a boy, Freddy was told:

> ONE DAY YOU WILL SEE A GHOSTLY WHITE LADY. THAT IS A SURE SIGN YOU ARE GOING TO DIE

He grew up and married the slightly potty Sophia. One night Sophia went on a sleep-walk in her white nightie.

She crashed through the glass door into Fred's bedroom. He awoke to see a white lady, splattered in blood, standing in his room. *The* white lady?

The shock was so great that he had a heart attack and never recovered.

A few days later he told the court, 'Today I am going to die.'

And he did.

Alexander 'The Wolf' of Badenoch in Scotland (1343–1405)

Legend has it that Alex died after a game of chess with his old friend the Devil.

Alex had been visited at Ruthven Castle by a tall man dressed in black. The man offered to play chess with the Wolf.

The game went on for several hours, until finally the tall man moved one of the chess pieces and called 'Checkmate – you lose.'

The man rose from the table. That night there was a massive storm of thunder, hail and lightning that went on for several hours.

161

Next morning an eerie silence fell.

Servants tiptoed into the hall. The stranger was gone. Alex's guards were found outside the castle walls dead and blackened as if they had all been hit by the lightning.

The Wolf was found in the main hall. His dead body was not marked, but the nails in his boots had all been torn out.

Benito Mussolini of Italy (1883–1945)

In 1939 Mussolini had led Italy to war – and defeat – in support of Hitler's Germany. The people who hated him most were his own subjects – the Freedom Fighters or 'Partisans' as they were known. He would be safe as long as he stayed out of their hands.

But his escape was ruined by a silly mistake.

It was an Esso petrol station.

You really wanted to know that, didn't you?

King Gustavus Adolphus of Sweden (1594–1632)

Of course, some leaders died in battle. Take Gustavus Adolphus of Sweden...

In 1632 Great Gus marched across Germany and smashed Pomerania and Mecklenburg.

Then he came to Lützen.

In the Battle of Lützen the King was shot in the back.

Gus's foot was caught in his horse's saddle and he was dragged along. Eventually his foot came free and he lay there, just about alive.

THE LION IS LYING!

His enemies finished him off with a shot through the head.

Next morning he was found face down in the mud. His body had been robbed of everything except his shirt.

NOW WHO WOULD DO A THING LIKE THAT, EH?

Maximilien François Marie Isidore de Robespierre of France (1758–1794)

Talking of messy, Monsieur Robespierre was another who died with blood on his face.

Little Max led the French Revolution while the 'Terror' reigned. Posh people lost their heads at the guillotine.

Noble noddles fell into a basket and were carted away.

Lop and plop! Lop and plop! Non-stop lop and plop. (Try saying that with a mouth full of mushrooms.)

165

Horrible Histories fascinating fact:
Many history books say:
'Robespierre, the man who sent tens of thousands to the guillotine, ended the same way.'

Tell your teacher:
1) Yes, thousands died, but Max himself only ordered 72 executions. (Not a lot of people know that.)
2) No he did *not* end the same way! The others were chopped in the neck by the guillotine. Max Robespierre was executed *face up* – chopped in the throat.

And there is a history mystery about Max's end.

Max was in a room with his friends when he heard his enemies were coming to get him. Some of his friends tried to kill themselves by jumping out of the window, but they ended up in the toilet pit below. Alive and very smelly.

Max Robespierre was dragged out by a French policeman called Charles Meda.

When they found him Max's jaw was hanging off, tied up with a bloody rag. He had been shot. But how did it happen?

There are three stories.
1) Robespierre tried to shoot himself. The bullet tore his jaw but didn't kill him.
2) Robespierre drew a gun. Brave Meda shot him in the jaw and arrested him.
3) Robespierre gave himself up and asked to speak to the people. Meda was told to shoot him in the jaw so he couldn't speak.

TOFFEE?

The truth? We may never know.

A report at the time described the horror of his execution.

166

Robespierre lies on a table, a wooden box for a pillow. Guards bully him, insult him; he speaks no word. His stockings have fallen down over his ankles.

At four in the afternoon the streets of Paris have never been so crowded. The streets are one dense stirring mass; all windows crammed; the roofs are filled with prying humans all with a strange gladness.

The death-carts roll on. All eyes are on Robespierre's cart, where he lies with his jaw bound in dirty linen. His half-dead brother lies beside him, their agony about to end.

A woman springs on the cart and cries, 'Your death makes me glad. Go down to hell with the curses of all wives and mothers!' At the foot of the scaffold, they stretch him on the ground till his turn comes. As he is lifted aloft his eyes open again and see the bloody blade.

Executioner Samsan tears off his coat, rips the dirty linen from his jaw. The jaw falls powerless, he gives a cry: hideous to hear and see. The blade falls and the crowd gives a shout of applause. A shout that rang out over Paris, over France, over Europe.

May God be merciful to him, and to us.

You get the feeling the French people didn't really like him.

Emperor Caligula of Rome (AD 12–41)

Caligula was cruel and vicious. It was no surprise that there were plots to kill him.

At last one plot worked. The leader was Cassius Chaerea, an officer in the royal guard, who hated Caligula. Why?

One night Chaerea trapped Caligula at the theatre, swung his sword and hacked open the Emperor's jaw.

Wounded Caligula made a run for his palace. A friend of Chaerea tripped the Emperor up.

More plotters rushed forward and started to stab Caligula. They kept going long after he was dead.

It was said that some even sank their teeth into his flesh.

Of course his wife and daughter were killed, too.

General Reinhard Heydrich of Germany (1904–1942)

Nasty Nazi Heydrich was nicknamed "The Hangman" because of his cruel treatment of his enemies. He made a big mistake – and it cost him his life.

Heydrich was one of the Nazis who planned the death camps that murdered six million people. Adolf Hitler sent him to rule Bohemia and Moravia for the Nazis.

His rule was so cruel that a team of Czech agents set out to assassinate him. They waited at a sharp bend in the road. When his car slowed down, an assassin jumped out, aimed his machine gun and pulled the trigger.

It didn't work![14] Oooops!

Luckily for the assassins another man had a tank bomb that he threw at the car. Heydrich was badly hurt.

The best Nazi doctors were sent to help him but he died a week later.

What killed him?

a) loss of blood
b) germs from the bomb
c) poisoned medicine

14 The men were trained in Britain and given British guns – ones that didn't work. Somehow Britain won the war. How?

Answer: **b)** The bomb was dirty and germs on the splinters poisoned Heydrich's blood.

Was Mr Hitler angry?

Yes – he was angry with the Czechs. He sent his troops to massacre every man over the age of 16 in the nearby town of Lidice.

But he was *also* angry with Heydrich for getting himself killed! At the funeral Hitler said:

Driving in an open, unarmoured vehicle is just damned foolishness, which does not help Germany one little bit. A man as important as Heydrich should not leave himself open to danger. I can only say he was stupid and idiotic.

That's all you need – you get assassinated then told it was your own fault!

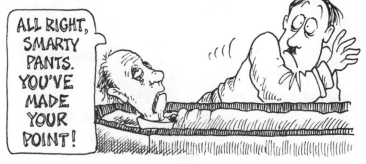

ALL RIGHT, SMARTY PANTS. YOU'VE MADE YOUR POINT!

Tsar Nicholas II of Russia (1868–1918)

If you kill a ruler then there is always the chance their children will grow up and seek revenge. So it's best to kill the whole family, not just the ruler.

That's what the Russians decided in 1918.

The royal Romanov family were taken to a cellar, lined up in two rows and shot by the secret police.

Their bodies were taken to old wells and mine shafts, where they were soaked with acid and burned on bonfires.

All that was found were a few jewels, false teeth, metal corsets – and a thumb.

But the thumb belonged to the family doctor.

EPILOGUE

What are leaders *for*? Do we really need them?

Rulers are supposed to care for their people. They don't.

In 1603 the plague ravaged London. What did caring Queen Elizabeth I do? She ran off to Windsor Castle, away from the disease in the city. Could her people do the same? No. Elizabeth had a gallows built and said:

Rulers are supposed to listen to their people. They don't.

Empress Anne of Russia liked to think of ways to punish her people. Did she listen to them if they complained about that punishment? No – because she had their tongues ripped out.

Rulers are supposed to set us an example. They only set us *bad* examples!

Peter III of Russia was a collector – he collected pickled nasties in jars. These included the pickled body of a two-headed child, the pickled body of a five-legged lamb, and the pickled head of a maidservant he'd had executed.

The pickle collection was looked after by a dwarf. When the dwarf died Peter had him pickled and put in a jar beside the rest.

Would *you* follow that example?

Some people have tried to tell rulers what to do.

A Roman writer called Onasander said:

A leader should go into battle with his people and share their danger.

He should praise the brave ...

... bully the cowards ...

... and drive on the lazy.

But not many rulers have done that.

Instead, they have hidden behind bodyguards and given cruel orders.

Rotten Rulers didn't have to get their hands dirty when they tortured and killed. Who did the bloody beheading, shocking shooting and horrible hanging? Not the ruler. It was the ruled.

Rotten Rulers can only win when the ordinary people do the cutting and the killing, the chopping and the lopping.

Ordinary people – like you and me. Mr and Ms Ordinary.

We remember people like Ivan the Terrible. But when Ivan had his minister boiled till his skin peeled off, Ivan didn't do the dipping.

Mr Ordinary did that.

When Russian ruler Joseph Stalin sent his secret police to arrest and execute 20 million people, what did Mr and Ms Ordinary do?

Nothing. They shut their doors, drew the curtains, shut out the horrors and let their neighbours die.

When your Rotten Ruler tells you to kill and die for them, what will *you* say, you ordinary person?

Horrible Histories:
The Savage Stone Age
The Awesome Egyptians
The Groovy Greeks
The Rotten Romans
The Ruthless Romans
The Cut-throat Celts
The Smashing Saxons
The Vicious Vikings
The Stormin' Normans
The Angry Aztecs
The Incredible Incas
The Measly Middle Ages
The Terrible Tudors
Even More Terrible Tudors
The Slimy Stuarts
The Gorgeous Georgians
The Vile Victorians
The Villainous Victorians
The Barmy British Empire
The Frightful First World War
The Woeful Second World War
The Blitzed Brits
Loathsome London

Horrible Histories Specials:
Bloody Scotland
Cruel Kings and Mean Queens
Dark Knights and Dingy Castles
England
France
Ireland
Rowdy Revolutions
The 20th Century
The USA
Wicked Words

Also available:
Cruel Crime and Painful Punishment
Dreadful Diary
The Wicked History of the World
The Mad Miscellany